POETS OF THE SOUTH

POETS OF THE SOUTH

A SERIES OF

BIOGRAPHICAL AND CRITICAL STUDIES

WITH

TYPICAL POEMS, ANNOTATED

BY

F. V. N. PAINTER, A.M., D.D.

Granger Index Reprint Series

BOOKS FOR LIBRARIES PRESS
FREEPORT, NEW YORK

First Published 1903
Reprinted 1968

PS 261
.P3
1968

LIBRARY OF CONGRESS CATALOG CARD NUMBER:

68-57064

MANUFACTURED
BY
HALLMARK LITHOGRAPHERS, INC.
IN THE U.S.A.

PREFACE

THE poets of the South, who constitute a worthy galaxy of poetic talent and achievement, are not sufficiently known. Even in the South, which might naturally be expected to take pride in its gifted singers, most of them, it is to be feared, are but little read.

This has been called an age of prose. Under the sway of what are regarded as "practical interests," there is a drifting away from poetic sentiment and poetic truth. This tendency is to be regretted, for material prosperity is never at its best without the grace and refinements of true culture. At the present time, as in former ages, the gifted poet is a seer, who reveals to us what is highest and best in life.

There is at present a new interest in literature in the South. The people read more; and in recent years an encouraging number of Southern writers have achieved national distinction. With this literary renaissance, there has been a turning back to older authors.

It is hoped that this little volume will supply a real need. It is intended to call fresh attention to the poetic achievement of the South. While minor poets are not forgotten, among whose writings is found many a gem of poetry, it is the leaders of the chorus — Poe, Hayne, Timrod, Lanier, and Ryan — who receive chief consideration. It may be doubted whether several of them have been given the place in American letters to which their gifts and achievements justly entitle them. It is hoped that the following biographical and critical sketches of these men, each highly gifted in his own way, will lead to a more careful reading of their works, in which, be it said to their honor, there is no thought or sentiment unworthy of a refined and chivalrous nature.

F. V. N. PAINTER.

SALEM, VIRGINIA.

CONTENTS

POETS OF THE SOUTH

CHAPTER I

MINOR POETS OF THE SOUTH

THE first poetic writer of this country had his home at Jamestown. He was **George Sandys** who came to Virginia in 1621, and succeeded his brother as treasurer of the newly established colony. Amid the hardships of pioneer colonial life, in which he proved himself a leading spirit, he had the literary zeal to complete his translation of Ovid's *Metamorphoses*, which he had begun in England. After the toilsome day, spent in introducing iron works or in encouraging shipbuilding, he sat down at night, within the shadow of surrounding forests, to construct his careful, rhymed pentameters. The conditions under which he wrote were very far removed from the Golden Age which he described, —

"Which uncompelled
And without rule, in faith and truth, excelled."

The promise of this bright, heroic beginning in poetry was not realized ; and scarcely another voice was heard in verse in the South before the Revolution.

The type of civilization developed in the South prior to the Civil War, admirable as it was in many other particulars, was hardly favorable to literature. The energies of the most intelligent portion of the population were directed to agriculture or to politics; and many of the foremost statesmen of our country — men like Washington, Jefferson, Marshall, Calhoun, Benton — were from the Southern states. The system of slavery, while building up baronial homes of wealth, culture, and boundless hospitality, checked manufacture, retarded the growth of cities, and turned the tide of immigration westward. Without a vigorous public school system, a considerable part of the non-slaveholding class remained without literary taste or culture.

The South has been chiefly an agricultural region, and has adhered to conservative habits of thought. While various movements in theology, philosophy, and literature were stirring New England, the South pursued the even tenor of its way. Of all parts of our country, it has been most tenacious of old customs and beliefs. Before the Civil War the cultivated classes of the Southern states found their intellectual nourishment in the older English classics, and Pope, Addison, and Shakespeare formed a part of every gentleman's library. There were no great publishing houses to stimulate literary production; and to this day Southern writers are dependent chiefly on Northern publishers to give their works to the public. Literature was hardly taken seriously; it was rather regarded, to use the words of Paul Hamilton Hayne, "as the choice recreation of gentlemen, as something fair and good, to be courted in a dainty, amateur fashion, and illustrated by *apropos* quotations from Lucretius, Virgil, or Horace." Thus it happened that before the Civil War literature in the South, whether prose or poetry, had a less vigorous development than in the Middle States and New England.

Yet it has been common to undervalue the literary work of the South. While literature was not generally encouraged there before the Civil War, — a fact lamented by gifted, representative writers, — there were at least two literary centers that exerted a notable influence. The first was Richmond, the home of Poe during his earlier years, and of the *Southern Literary Messenger*, in its day the most influential magazine south of the Potomac. It was founded, as set forth in its first issue, in 1834, to encourage literature in Virginia and the other states of the South ; and during its career of twenty-eight years it stimulated literary activity in a remarkable degree. Among its contributors we find Poe, Simms, Hayne, Timrod, John Esten Cooke, John R. Thompson, and others — a galaxy of the best-known names in Southern literature.

The other principal literary center of the South was Charleston. "Legaré's wit and scholarship," to adopt the words of Mrs. Margaret J. Preston, "brightened its social circle ; Calhoun's deep shadow loomed over it from his plantation at Fort Hill ; Gilmore Simms's genial culture broadened its sympathies. The latter was the Mæcenas to a band of brilliant youths who used to meet for literary suppers at his beautiful home." Among these brilliant youths were Paul Hamilton Hayne and Henry Timrod, two of the best poets the South has produced. The *Southern Literary Gazette*, founded by Simms, and *Russell's Magazine*, edited by Hayne, were published at Charleston. Louisville and New Orleans were likewise literary centers of more or less influence.

Yet it is a notable fact that none of these literary centers gave rise to a distinctive group or school of writers. The influence of these centers did not consist in one great dominating principle, but in a general stimulus to literary effort. In this respect it may be fairly claimed that the South was more cosmopolitan than the North. In New England, theology and transcendentalism in turn dominated literature; and not a few of the group of writers who contributed to the *Atlantic Monthly* were profoundly influenced by the anti-slavery agitation. They struggled up Parnassus, to use the words of Lowell, —

"With a whole bale of *isms* tied together with rime."

But the leading writers of the South, as will be seen later, have been exempt, in large measure, from the narrowing influence of one-sided theological or philosophical tenets. They have not aspired to the rôle of social reformers; and in their loyalty to art, they have abstained from fanatical energy and extravagance.

The major poets of the South stand out in strong, isolated individuality. They were not bound together by any sympathy other than that of a common interest in art and in their Southern home. Their genius was nourished on the choicest literary productions of England and of classic antiquity; and looking, with this Old World culture, upon Southern landscape and Southern character, they pictured or interpreted them in the language of poetry.

The three leading poets of the Civil War period — Hayne, Timrod, and Ryan — keenly felt the issues involved in that great struggle. All three of them were connected, for a time at least, with the Confederate army. In the earlier stages of the conflict, the intensity of their Southern feeling flamed out in thrilling lyrics. Timrod's martial songs throb with the energy of deep emotion. But all three poets lived to accept the results of the war, and to sing a new loyalty to our great Republic.

The South has not been as unfruitful in literature as is often supposed. While there have been very few to make literature a vocation, a surprisingly large number have made it an avocation. Law and literature, as we shall have occasion to note, have frequently gone hand in hand. A recent work on Southern literature [1] enumerates more than twelve hundred writers, most of whom have published one or more volumes. There are more than two hundred poets who have been thought worthy of mention. More than fifty poets have been credited to Virginia alone; and an examination of their works reveals, among a good deal that is commonplace and imitative, many a little

[1] Manly's *Southern Literature*.

gem that ought to be preserved. Apart from the five major poets of the South — Poe, Hayne, Timrod, Lanier, and Ryan — who are reserved for special study, we shall now consider a few of the minor poets who have produced verse of excellent quality.

Francis Scott Key (1780–1843) is known throughout the land as the author of *The Star-spangled Banner*, the noblest, perhaps, of our patriotic hymns. He was born in Frederick County, Maryland, and was educated at St. John's College, Annapolis. He studied law, and after practicing with success in Frederick City, he removed to Washington, where he became district attorney.

During the bombardment of Fort McHenry in the War of 1812, he was detained on board a British vessel, whither he had gone to secure the release of a friend. All night long he watched the bombardment with the keenest anxiety. In the morning, when the dawn disclosed the star-spangled banner still proudly waving over the fort, he conceived the stirring song, which at once became popular and was sung all over the country. Though a volume of his poems, with a sketch by Chief-Justice Taney, was published in 1857, it is to *The Star-spangled Banner* that he owes his literary fame.

"O say, can you see, by the dawn's early light,
    What so proudly we hailed at the twilight's last
        gleaming,
  Whose broad stripes and bright stars through the
        perilous fight
    O'er the ramparts we watched, were so gallantly
        streaming?

And the rockets' red glare, the bombs bursting in air,
Gave proof through the night that our flag was still
    there.
O say, does that star-spangled banner yet wave
O'er the land of the free and the home of the brave?"

Few poems written in the South have been more
popular than *My Life is like the Summer Rose*.
It has the distinction of having been praised by
Byron. Its author, **Richard Henry Wilde** (1789–
1847), was born in Dublin, Ireland, but brought up
and educated in Augusta, Georgia. He studied
law, became attorney general of his adopted state,
and later entered Congress, where he served for
several terms. He was a man of scholarly tastes
and poetic gifts. He spent five years abroad,
chiefly in Italy, where his studies in Italian literature afterwards led to a work on Torquato Tasso.
It was on the occasion of this trip abroad that he
wrote *A Farewell to America*, which breathes a
noble spirit of patriotism: —

" Farewell, my more than fatherland!
    Home of my heart and friends, adieu!
Lingering beside some foreign strand,
    How oft shall I remember you!
    How often, o'er the waters blue,
Send back a sigh to those I leave,
    The loving and beloved few,
Who grieve for me, — for whom I grieve!"

On his return to America, he settled in New
Orleans, where he became a professor of law in the
University of Louisiana. Though the author of

a volume of poems of more than usual excellence, it is the melancholy lyric, *My Life is like the Summer Rose*, that, more than all the rest, has given him a niche in the temple of literary fame. Is it necessary to quote a stanza of a poem so well known?

> " My life is like the summer rose,
>   That opens to the morning sky,
> But, ere the shades of evening close,
>   Is scattered on the ground — to die!
> Yet on the rose's humble bed
> The sweetest dews of night are shed,
> As if she wept the waste to see —
> But none shall weep a tear for me! "

George D. Prentice (1802–1870) was a native of Connecticut. He was educated at Brown University, and studied law; but he soon gave up his profession for the more congenial pursuit of literature. In 1828 he established at Hartford the *New England Weekly Review*, in which a number of his poems, serious and sentimental, appeared. Two years later, at the age of twenty-eight, he turned over his paper to Whittier and removed to Louisville, where he became editor of the *Journal*.

He was a man of brilliant intellect, and soon made his paper a power in education, society, and politics. Apart from his own vigorous contributions, he made his paper useful to Southern letters by encouraging literary activity in others. It was chiefly through his influence that Louisville became one of the literary centers of the South. He was a stout opponent of secession; and when the Civil War came his paper, like his adopted state, suffered severely.

Among his writings is a *Life of Henry Clay.* A collection of his witty and pungent paragraphs has also been published under the title of *Prenticeana.* His poems, by which he will be longest remembered, were collected after his death. His best-known poem is *The Closing Year.* Though its vividness and eloquence are quite remarkable, its style is, perhaps, too declamatory for the taste of the present generation. The following lines, which express the poet's bright hopes for the political future of the world, are taken from *The Flight of Years:* —

> "Weep not, that Time
> Is passing on — it will ere long reveal
> A brighter era to the nations. Hark!
> Along the vales and mountains of the earth
> There is a deep, portentous murmuring
> Like the swift rush of subterranean streams,
> Or like the mingled sounds of earth and air,
> When the fierce Tempest, with sonorous wing,
> Heaves his deep folds upon the rushing winds,
> And hurries onward with his night of clouds
> Against the eternal mountains. 'Tis the voice
> Of infant *Freedom* — and her stirring call
> Is heard and answered in a thousand tones
> From every hilltop of her western home —
> And lo — it breaks across old Ocean's flood —
> And *Freedom, Freedom!* is the answering shout
> Of nations starting from the spell of years.

The dayspring!—see—'tis brightening in the heavens!
The watchmen of the night have caught the sign —
From tower to tower the signal fires flash free —
And the deep watchword, like the rush of seas
That heralds the volcano's bursting flame,
Is sounding o'er the earth.   Bright years of hope
And life are on the wing. — Yon glorious bow
Of Freedom, bended by the hand of God,
Is spanning Time's dark surges.   Its high arch,
A type of love and mercy on the cloud,
Tells that the many storms of human life
Will pass in silence, and the sinking waves,
Gathering the forms of glory and of peace,
Reflect the undimmed brightness of the Heaven."

William Gilmore Simms (1806–1870), a native
of Charleston, was a man of remarkable versatility.   He made up for his lack of collegiate
training by private study and wide experience.
He early gave up law for literature, and during
his long and tireless literary career was editor,
poet, dramatist, historian, and novelist.   He had
something of the wideness of range of Sir Walter
Scott; and one can not but think that, had he lived
north of Mason and Dixon's line, he might occupy
a more prominent place in the literary annals of
our country.   He has been styled the "Cooper
of the South"; but it is hardly too much to say
that in versatility, culture, and literary produc-
tiveness he surpassed his great Northern contemporary.

Simms was a poet before he became a novelist.
The poetic impulse manifested itself early; and

before he was twenty-five he had published three or more volumes of verse. In 1832 his imaginative poem, *Atalantis, a Story of the Sea*, was brought out by the Harpers; and it introduced him at once to the favorable notice of what Poe called the "Literati" of New York. His subsequent volumes of poetry were devoted chiefly to a description of Southern scenes and incidents.

As will be seen in our studies of Hayne and Timrod, Simms was an important figure in the literary circles of Charleston. His large, vigorous nature seemed incapable of jealousy, and he took delight in lending encouragement to young men of literary taste and aspiration. He was a laborious and prolific writer, the number of his various works — poetry, drama, history, fiction — reaching nearly a hundred. Had he written less rapidly, his work might have gained, perhaps, in artistic quality.

Among the best of Simms's novels is a series devoted to the Revolution. The characters and incidents of that conflict in South Carolina are graphically portrayed. *The Partisan*, the first of this historic series, was published in 1835. *The Yemassee* is an Indian story, in which the character of the red man is less idealized than in Cooper's *Leatherstocking Tales*. In *The Damsel of Darien*, the hero is Balboa, the discoverer of the Pacific.

The verse of Simms is characterized by facile vigor rather than by fine poetic quality. The following lines, which represent his style at its best, bear a lesson for the American people to-day : —

" This the true sign of ruin to a race —
    It undertakes no march, and day by day
Drowses in camp, or, with the laggard's pace,
    Walks sentry o'er possessions that decay ;
    Destined, with sensible waste, to fleet away ; —
For the first secret of continued power
    Is the continued conquest ; — all our sway
Hath surety in the uses of the hour ;
If that we waste, in vain walled town and lofty tower ! "

Edward Coate Pinkney (1802–1828) died before his poetic gifts had reached their full maturity. He was the son of the eminent lawyer and diplomatist, William Pinkney, and was born in London, while his father was American minister at the court of St. James. At the age of nine he was brought home to America, and educated at Baltimore. He spent eight years in the United States navy, during which period he visited the classic shores of the Mediterranean. He was impressed particularly with the beauty of Italy, and in one of his poems he says : —

" It looks a dimple on the face of earth,
    The seal of beauty, and the shrine of mirth ;
    Nature is delicate and graceful there,
    The place's genius feminine and fair :
    The winds are awed, nor dare to breathe aloud ;
    The air seems never to have borne a cloud,
    Save where volcanoes send to heaven their curled
    And solemn smokes, like altars of the world."

In 1824 he resigned his place in the navy to take up the practice of law in Baltimore. His health was not good; and he seems to have occupied a part of his abundant leisure (for he was not successful in his profession) in writing poetry. A thin volume of poems was published in 1825, in which he displays, especially in his shorter pieces, an excellent lyrical gift. The following stanzas are from *A Health:* —

> " I fill this cup to one made up
>   Of loveliness alone,
> A woman, of her gentle sex
>   The seeming paragon;
> To whom the better elements
>   And kindly stars have given
> A form so fair, that, like the air,
>   'Tis less of earth than heaven.

> " Her every tone is music's own,
>   Like those of morning birds,
> And something more than melody
>   Dwells ever in her words;
> The coinage of her heart are they,
>   And from her lips each flows
> As one may see the burdened bee
>   Forth issue from the rose."

Philip Pendleton Cooke (1816–1850), like most Southern writers before the Civil War, mingled literature with the practice of law. He was born at Martinsburg, Virginia, and educated at Princeton. He early manifested a literary bent, and wrote for the *Knickerbocker Magazine,* the oldest of our literary monthlies, before he was out of his teens.   He was noted for his love of outdoor life, and became a thorough sportsman.   In 1847 he published a volume entitled *Froissart Ballads and Other Poems*.   The origin of the ballad portion of the volume, as explained in the preface, is found in the lines of an old Roman poet : —

" A certain freak has got into my head,
      Which I can't conquer for the life of me,
   Of taking up some history, little read,
      Or known, and writing it in poetry."

The best known of his lyrics is *Florence Vane* which has the sincerity and pathos of a real experience : —

   " I loved thee long and dearly,
         Florence Vane ;
      My life's bright dream, and early,
         Hath come again ;
      I renew, in my fond vision,
         My heart's dear pain,
      My hope, and thy derision,
         Florence Vane.

   " The ruin lone and hoary,
         The ruin old,
      Where thou didst hark my story,
         At even told, —
      That spot — the hues Elysian
         Of sky and plain —
      I treasure in my vision,
         Florence Vane.

> " Thou wast lovelier than the roses
>   In their prime ;
> Thy voice excelled the closes
>   Of sweetest rhyme ;
> Thy heart was as a river
>   Without a main.
> Would I had loved thee never,
>   Florence Vane ! "

Theodore O'Hara (1820–1867) is chiefly remembered for a single poem that has touched the national heart. He was born in Danville, Kentucky. After taking a course in law, he accepted a clerkship in the Treasury Department at Washington. On the outbreak of the Mexican War he enlisted as a private soldier, and by his gallant service rose to the rank of captain and major. After the close of the war he returned to Washington and engaged for a time in the practice of his profession. Later he became editor of the *Mobile Register*, and *Frankfort Yeoman* in Kentucky. In the Civil War he served as colonel in the Confederate army.

The poem on which his fame largely rests is *The Bivouac of the Dead*. It was written to commemorate the Kentuckians who fell in the battle of Buena Vista. Its well-known lines have furnished an apt inscription for several military cemeteries : —

> " The muffled drum's sad roll has beat
>   The soldier's last tattoo ;
> No more on Life's parade shall meet
>   That brave and fallen few.

> On Fame's eternal camping-ground
>   Their silent tents are spread,
> And Glory guards, with solemn round,
>   The bivouac of the dead."

O'Hara died in Alabama in 1867. The legislature of Kentucky paid him a fitting tribute in having his body removed to Frankfort and placed by the side of the heroes whom he so worthily commemorated in his famous poem.

Francis Orrery Ticknor (1822–1874) was a physician living near Columbus, Georgia. He led a busy, useful, humble life, and his merits as a poet have not been fully recognized. In the opinion of Paul Hamilton Hayne, who edited a volume of Ticknor's poems, he was "one of the truest and sweetest lyric poets this country has yet produced." *The Virginians of the Valley* was written after the soldiers of the Old Dominion, many of whom bore the names of the knights of the "Golden Horseshoe," had obtained a temporary advantage over the invading forces of the North : —

> " We thought they slept ! — the sons who kept
>   The names of noble sires,
> And slumbered while the darkness crept
>   Around their vigil fires ;
> But aye the " Golden Horseshoe " knights
>   Their Old Dominion keep,
> Whose foes have found enchanted ground,
>   But not a knight asleep."

But a martial lyric of greater force is *Little Giffen*, written in honor of a blue-eyed lad of

East Tennessee. He was terribly wounded in some engagement, and after being taken to the hospital at Columbus, Georgia, was finally nursed back to life in the home of Dr. Ticknor. Beneath the thin, insignificant exterior of the lad, the poet discerned the incarnate courage of the hero : —

" Out of the focal and foremost fire,
  Out of the hospital walls as dire ;
  Smitten of grape-shot and gangrene,
  (Eighteenth battle and *he* sixteen !)
  Specter ! such as you seldom see,
  Little Giffen of Tennessee !

* * * * * *

" Word of gloom from the war, one day ;
  Johnson pressed at the front, they say.
  Little Giffen was up and away ;
  A tear — his first — as he bade good-by,
  Dimmed the glint of his steel-blue eye.
  ' I'll write, if spared ! ' There was news of the fight ;
  But none of Giffen. — He did not write."

But Ticknor did not confine himself to war themes. He was a lover of Nature ; and its forms, and colors, and sounds — as seen in *April Morning*, *Twilight*, *The Hills*, *Among the Birds* — appealed to his sensitive nature. Shut out from literary centers and literary companionship, he sang, like Burns, from the strong impulse awakened by the presence of the heroic and the beautiful.

John R. Thompson (1823-1873) has deserved well of the South both as editor and author. He was born in Richmond, and educated at the University

of Virginia, where he received the degree of Bache-
lor of Arts in 1845.   Two years later he became
editor of the *Southern Literary Messenger;* and
during the twelve years of his editorial management, he not only maintained a high degree of
literary excellence, but took pains to lend encouragement to Southern letters.   It is a misfortune
to our literature that his writings, particularly his
poetry, have never been collected.

The incidents of the Civil War called forth many
a stirring lyric, the best of which is his well-known
Music in Camp : —

> " Two armies covered hill and plain,
>   Where Rappahannock's waters
> Ran deeply crimsoned with the stain
>   Of battle's recent slaughters."

The band had played "Dixie" and "Yankee
Doodle," which in turn had been greeted with
shouts by "Rebels" and "Yanks."

> " And yet once more the bugles sang
>   Above the stormy riot;
> No shout upon the evening rang —
>   There reigned a holy quiet.

> " The sad, slow stream its noiseless flood
>   Poured o'er the glistening pebbles;
> All silent now the Yankees stood,
>   And silent stood the Rebels.

> " No unresponsive soul had heard
>   That plaintive note's appealing,
> So deeply ' Home, Sweet Home ' had stirred
>   The hidden founts of feeling.

"Or Blue or Gray, the soldier sees,
    As by the wand of fairy,
The cottage 'neath the live-oak trees,
    The cabin by the prairie."

On account of failing health, Thompson made a
visit to Europe, where he spent several years, con-
tributing from time to time to *Blackwood's Magazine* and other English periodicals.   On his return
to America, he was engaged on the editorial staff
of the *New York Evening Post*, with which he was
connected till his death, in 1873.   He is buried in
Hollywood cemetery at Richmond.

"The city's hum drifts o'er his grave,
    And green above the hollies wave
Their jagged leaves, as when a boy,
    On blissful summer afternoons,
    He came to sing the birds his runes,
And tell the river of his joy."

The verse of Mrs. Margaret J. Preston (1820–
1897) rises above the commonplace both in sentiment and craftsmanship.   She belongs, as some
critic has said, to the school of Mrs. Browning;
and in range of subject and purity of sentiment
she is scarcely inferior to her great English contemporary.   She was the daughter of the Rev.
George Junkin, D.D., the founder of Lafayette
College, Pennsylvania, and for many years president of Washington College at Lexington, Virginia.
In 1857 she married Colonel J. T. L. Preston of
the Virginia Military Institute.

For many years she was a contributor to the *Southern Literary Messenger,* in which her earlier poems first made their appearance. Though a native of Philadelphia, she was loyal to the South during the Civil War, and found inspiration in its deeds of heroism. *Beechen-brook* is a rhyme of the war; and though well-nigh forgotten now, it was read, on its publication in 1865, from the Potomac to the Gulf. Among her other writings are *Old Songs and New* and *Cartoons.* Her poetry is pervaded by a deeply religious spirit, and she repeatedly urges the lesson of supreme resignation and trust, as in the following lines : —

" What will it matter by-and-by
　　Whether my path below was bright,
　　Whether it wound through dark or light,
　Under a gray or golden sky,
　When I look back on it, by-and-by ?

" What will it matter by-and-by
　　Whether, unhelped, I toiled alone,
　　Dashing my foot against a stone,
　Missing the charge of the angel nigh,
　Bidding me think of the by-and-by ?

　　　　*　　*　　*　　*　　*

" What will it matter ?　Naught, if I
　　Only am sure the way I've trod,
　　Gloomy or gladdened, leads to God,
　Questioning not of the how, the why,
　If I but reach Him by-and-by.

" What will I care for the unshared sigh,
　　If in my fear of lapse or fall,
　　Close I have clung to Christ through all,

Mindless how rough the road might lie,
Sure He will smoothen it by-and-by.

" What will it matter by-and-by?
    Nothing but this : that Joy or Pain
    Lifted me skyward, — helped me to gain,
    Whether through rack, or smile, or sigh,
    Heaven, home, all in all, by-and-by."

In this rapid sketch of the minor singers of the South, it has been necessary to omit many names worthy of mention. It is beyond our scope to speak of the newer race of poets. Here and there delicate notes are heard, but there is no evidence that a great singer is present among us. Yet there is no ground for discouragement; the changed conditions and the new spirit that has come upon our people may reasonably be expected to lead to higher poetic achievement.

In some respects the South affords a more promising field for literature than any other part of our country. There is evident decadence in New England. But the climate and scenery, the history and traditions, and the chivalrous spirit and unexhausted intellectual energies of the South contain the promise of an Augustan age in literature. In no insignificant degree its rich-ored veins have been worked in prose. **Joel Chandler Harris** has successfully wrought in the mine of negro folk-lore; **George W. Cable** has portrayed the Creole life of Louisiana; **Charles Egbert Craddock** has pictured the types of character found among the Tennessee mountains; **Thomas Nelson Page** has shown us the trials and triumphs of Reconstruction days; and Miss **Mary Johnston** has revived the picturesque scenes of colonial times. There has been an obvious literary awakening in the South; and sooner or later it will find utterance, let us hope, in some strong-voiced, great-souled singer.

It is true that there are obstacles to be overcome. There are no literary magazines in the South to encourage and develop our native talent as in the days of the *Southern Literary Messenger.* Southern writers are still dependent upon Northern periodicals, in which they can hardly be said to find a cordial welcome. It seems that the South in a measure suffers the obloquy that rested of old upon Nazareth, from which the Pharisees of the metropolis maintained that no good thing could come.

But the most serious drawback of all is the disfavor into which poetry has fallen, or rather which it has brought upon itself. In the remoteness of its themes and sentiments, in its over-anxiety for a faultless or striking technique, it has erected a barrier between itself and the sanity of a practical, truth-loving people. Let us hope that this aberration is not permanent. When poetry returns to simplicity, sincerity, and truth; when it shall voice, as in the great English singers, Tennyson and Browning, the deepest thought and aspirations of our race; when once more, as in the prophetic days of old, it shall resume its lofty, seer-like office, — then will it be restored to its place of honor by a delighted and grateful people.

CHAPTER II

POE occupies a peculiar place in American literature. He has been called our most interesting literary man. He stands alone for his intellectual brilliancy and his lamentable failure to use it wisely. No one can read his works intelligently without being impressed with his extraordinary ability. Whether poetry, criticism, or fiction, he shows extraordinary power in them all. But the moral element in life is the most important, and in this Poe was lacking. With him truth was not the first necessity. He allowed his judgment to be warped by friendship, and apparently sacrificed sincerity to the vulgar desire of gaining popular applause. Through intemperate habits, he was unable for any considerable length of time to maintain himself in a responsible or lucrative position. Fortune repeatedly opened to him an inviting door ; but he constantly and ruthlessly abused her kindness.

Edgar Allan Poe descended from an honorable ancestry. His grandfather, David Poe, was a Revolutionary hero, over whose grave, as he kissed the sod, Lafayette pronounced the words, "*Ici repose un cœur noble.*" His father, an impulsive and wayward youth, fell in love with an English

EDGAR ALLAN POE.

actress, and forsook the bar for the stage. The couple were duly married, and acted with moderate success in the principal towns and cities of the country. It was during an engagement at Boston that the future poet was born, January 19, 1809. Two years later the wandering pair were again in Richmond, where within a few weeks of each other they died in poverty. They left three children, the second of whom, Edgar, was kindly received into the home of Mr. John Allan, a wealthy merchant of the city.

The early training of Poe was misguided and unfortunate. The boy was remarkably pretty and precocious, and his foster-parents allowed no opportunity to pass without showing him off. After dinner in this elegant and hospitable home, he was frequently placed upon the table to drink to the health of the guests, and to deliver short declamations, for which he had inherited a decided talent. He was flattered and fondled and indulged in every way. Is it strange that under this training he acquired a taste for strong drink, and became opinionated and perverse?

In 1815 Mr. Allan went to England with his family to spend several years, and there placed the young Edgar at school in an ancient and historic town, which has since been swallowed up in the overflow of the great metropolis. The venerable appearance and associations of the town, as may be learned from the autobiographic tale of *William Wilson*, made a deep and lasting impression on the imaginative boy.

After five years spent in this English school, where he learned to read Latin and to speak French, he was brought back to America, and placed in a Richmond academy. Without much diligence in study, his brilliancy enabled him to take high rank in his classes. His skill in verse-making and in debate made him prominent in the school. He excelled in athletic exercises, but was not generally popular among his fellow-students. Conscious of his superior intellectual endowments, he was disposed to live apart and indulge in moody reverie. According to the testimony of one who knew him well at this time, he was "self-willed, capricious, inclined to be imperious, and though of generous impulses, not steadily kind, or even amiable."

In 1826, at the age of seventeen, Poe matriculated at the University of Virginia, and entered the schools of ancient and modern languages. Though he attended his classes with a fair degree of regularity, he was not slow in joining the fast set. Gambling seems to have become a passion with him, and he lost heavily. His reckless expenditures led Mr. Allan to visit Charlottesville for the purpose of inquiring into his habits. The result appears not to have been satisfactory; and though his adopted son won high honors in Latin and French, Mr. Allan refused to allow him to return to the university after the close of his first session, and placed him in his own counting-room.

It is not difficult to foresee the next step in the drama before us. Many a genius of far greater self-restraint and moral earnestness has found the routine of business almost intolerably irksome. With high notions of his own ability, and with a temper rebellious to all restraint, Poe soon broke away from his new duties, and started out to seek his fortune. He went to Boston; and, in eager search for fame and money, he resorted to the rather unpromising expedient of publishing, in 1827, a small volume of poems. Viewed in the light of his subsequent career, the volume gives here and there an intimation of the author's genius; but, as was to be expected, it attracted but little attention. He was soon reduced to financial straits, and in his pressing need he enlisted, under an assumed name, in the United States army. He served at Fort Moultrie, and afterward at Fortress Monroe. He rose to the rank of sergeant major; and, according to the testimony of his superiors, he was "exemplary in his deportment, prompt and faithful in the discharge of his duties."

In 1829, when his heart was softened by the death of his wife, Mr. Allan became reconciled to his adopted but wayward son. Through his influence, young Poe secured a discharge from the army, and obtained an appointment as cadet at West Point. He entered the military academy July 1, 1830, and, as usual, established a reputation for brilliancy and folly. He was reserved, exclusive, discontented, and censorious. As described by a classmate, " He was an accomplished French scholar, and had a wonderful aptitude for mathematics, so that he had no difficulty in preparing his recitations in his class, and in obtaining the highest marks in these departments. He was a devourer of books; but his great fault was his neglect of and apparent contempt for military duties. His wayward and capricious temper made him at times utterly oblivious or indifferent to the ordinary routine of roll call, drills, and guard duties. These habits subjected him often to arrest and punishment, and effectually prevented his learning or discharging the duties of a soldier." The final result may be easily anticipated: at the end of six months, he was summoned before a court-martial, tried, and expelled.

Before leaving West Point, Poe arranged for the publication of a volume of poetry, which appeared in New York in 1831. This volume, to which the students of the academy subscribed liberally in advance, is noteworthy in several particulars. In a prefatory letter Poe lays down the poetic principle to which he endeavored to conform his productions. It throws much light on his poetry by exhibiting the ideal at which he aimed. "A poem, in my opinion," he says, "is opposed to a work of science by having for its *immediate* object pleasure, not truth; to romance, by having for its object an *indefinite* instead of a definite pleasure, being a poem only so far as this object is attained; romance presenting perceptible images with definite, poetry with *in*definite sensations, to which end music is an *essential*, since the comprehension of sweet sound is our most indefinite conception. Music, when

combined with a pleasurable idea, is poetry ; music
without the idea is simply music ; the idea without
the music is prose from its very definiteness."
Music embodied in a golden mist of thought and
sentiment — this is Poe's poetic ideal.

As illustrative of his musical rhythm, the following lines from *Al Aaraaf* may be given : —

> " Ligeia ! Ligeia !
>   My beautiful one !
> Whose harshest idea
>   Will to melody run,
> O ! is it thy will
>   On the breezes to toss ?
> Or, capriciously still,
>   Like the lone Albatross,
> Incumbent on night
>   (As she on the air)
> To keep watch with delight
>   On the harmony there ? "

Or take the last stanza of *Israfel :* —

> " If I could dwell
> Where Israfel
>   Hath dwelt, and he where I,
> He might not sing so wildly well
>   A mortal melody,
> While a bolder note than this might swell
>   From my lyre within the sky."

The two principal poems in the volume under
consideration — *Al Aaraaf* and *Tamerlane* — are
obvious imitations of Moore and Byron. The

beginning of *Al Aaraaf*, for example, might easily be mistaken for an extract from *Lalla Rookh*, so similar are the rhythm and rhyme : —

> " O ! nothing earthly save the ray
> (Thrown back from flowers) of Beauty's eye,
> As in those gardens where the day
> Springs from the gems of Circassy —
> O ! nothing earthly save the thrill
> Of melody in woodland rill —
> Or (music of the passion-hearted)
> Joy's voice so peacefully departed
> That, like the murmur in the shell,
> Its echo dwelleth and will dwell —
> Oh, nothing of the dross of ours —
> Yet all the beauty — all the flowers
> That list our Love, and deck our bowers —
> Adorn yon world afar, afar —
> The wandering star."

After his expulsion from West Point, Poe appears to have gone to Richmond; but the long-suffering of Mr. Allan, who had married àgain after the death of his first wife, was at length exhausted. He refused to extend any further recognition to one whom he had too much reason to regard as unappreciative and undeserving. Accordingly Poe was thrown upon his own resources for a livelihood. He settled in Baltimore, where he had a few acquaintances and friends, and entered upon that literary career which is without parallel in American literature for its achievements, its vicissitudes, and its sorrows. With no qualification for the struggle of life other than intellectual brilliancy, he bitterly atoned, through disappointment and suffering, for his defects of temper, lack of judgment, and habits of intemperance.

In 1833 the Baltimore *Saturday Visitor* offered a prize of one hundred dollars for the best prose story. This prize Poe won by his tale, *A Ms. Found in a Bottle.* This success may be regarded as the first step in his literary career. The ability displayed in this fantastic tale brought him to the notice of John P. Kennedy, Esq., who at once befriended him in his distress, and aided him in his literary projects. He gave Poe, whom he found in extreme poverty, free access to his home and, to use his own words, " brought him up from the very verge of despair."

After a year or more of hack work in Baltimore, Poe, through the influence of his kindly patron, obtained employment on the *Southern Literary Messenger*, and removed to Richmond in 1835. Here he made a brilliant start ; life seemed to open before him full of promise. In a short time he was promoted to the editorship of the *Messenger*, and by his tales, poems, and especially his reviews, he made that periodical very popular. In a twelve-month he increased its subscription list from seven hundred to nearly five thousand, and made the magazine a rival of the *Knickerbocker* and the *New Englander.* He was loudly praised by the Southern press, and was generally regarded as one of the foremost writers of the day.

In the *Messenger* Poe began his work as a critic. It is hardly necessary to say that his criticism was of the slashing kind. He became little short of a terror. With a great deal of critical acumen and a fine artistic sense, he made relentless war on pretentious mediocrity, and rendered good service to American letters by enforcing higher literary standards. He was lavish in his charges of plagiarism; and he made use of cheap, second-hand learning in order to ridicule the pretended scholarship of others. He often affected an irritating and contemptuous superiority. But with all his humbug and superciliousness, his critical estimates, in the main, have been sustained.

The bright prospects before Poe were in a few months ruthlessly blighted. Perhaps he relied too much on his genius and reputation. It is easy for men of ability to overrate their importance. Regarding himself, perhaps, as indispensable to the *Messenger*, he may have relaxed in vigilant self-restraint. It has been claimed that he resigned the editorship in order to accept a more lucrative offer in New York; but the sad truth seems to be that he was dismissed on account of his irregular habits.

After eighteen months in Richmond, during which he had established a brilliant literary reputation, Poe was again turned adrift. He went to New York, where his story, *The Adventures of Arthur Gordon Pym*, was published by the Harpers in 1838. It is a tale of the sea, written with the simplicity of style and circumstantiality of detail that give such charm to the works of Defoe. In spite of the fact that Cooper and Marryat had created a taste for sea-tales, this story never became popular. It is superabundant in horrors — a vein that had a fatal fascination for the morbid genius of Poe.

The same year in which this story appeared, Poe removed to Philadelphia, where he soon found work on the *Gentleman's Magazine*, recently established by the comedian Burton. He soon rose to the position of editor-in-chief, and his talents proved of great value to the magazine. His tales and critiques rapidly increased its circulation. But the actor, whose love of justice does him great credit, could not approve of his editor's sensational criticism. In a letter written when their cordial relations were interrupted for a time, Burton speaks very plainly and positively : "I cannot permit the magazine to be made a vehicle for that sort of severity which you think is so 'successful with the mob.' I am truly much less anxious about making a monthly 'sensation' than I am upon the point of fairness. . . . You say the people love havoc. I think they love justice." Poe did not profit by his experience at Richmond, and after a few months he was dismissed for neglect of duty.

He was out of employment but a short time. In November, 1840, *Graham's Magazine* was established, and Poe appointed editor. At no other period of his life did his genius appear to better advantage. Thrilling stories and trenchant criticisms followed one another in rapid succession.

His articles on autography and cryptology attracted widespread attention. In the former he attempted to illustrate character by the handwriting; and in the latter he maintained that human ingenuity cannot invent a cipher that human ingenuity cannot resolve. In the course of a few months the circulation of the magazine (if its own statements may be trusted) increased from eight thousand to forty thousand — a remarkable circulation for that time.

His criticism was based on the rather violent assumption "that, as a literary people, we are one vast perambulating humbug." In most cases, he asserted, literary prominence was achieved "by the sole means of a blustering arrogance, or of a busy wriggling conceit, or of the most bare-faced plagiarism, or even through the simple immensity of its assumptions." These fraudulent reputations he undertook, "with the help of a hearty good will" (which no one will doubt) "to tumble down." He admitted that there were a few who rose above absolute "idiocy." "Mr. Bryant is not *all* a fool. Mr. Willis is not *quite* an ass. Mr. Longfellow *will* steal but, perhaps, he cannot help it (for we have heard of such things), and then it must not be denied that *nil tetigit quod non ornavit.*" But, in spite of such reckless and extravagant assertion, there was still too much acumen and force in his reviews for them to be treated with indifference or contempt.

In about eighteen months Poe's connection with Graham was dissolved. The reason has not been made perfectly clear; but from what we already know, it is safe to charge it to Poe's infirmity of temper or of habit. His protracted sojourn in Philadelphia was now drawing to a close. It had been the most richly productive, as well as the happiest, period of his life. For a time, sustained by appreciation and hope, he in a measure overcame his intemperate habits. Griswold, his much-abused biographer, has given us an interesting description of him and his home at this time: "His manner, except during his fits of intoxication, was very quiet and gentlemanly; he was usually dressed with simplicity and elegance; and when once he sent for me to visit him, during a period of illness caused by protracted and anxious watching at the side of his sick wife, I was impressed by the singular neatness and the air of refinement in his home. It was in a small house, in one of the pleasant and silent neighborhoods far from the center of the town; and, though slightly and cheaply furnished, everything in it was so tasteful and so fitly disposed that it seemed altogether suitable for a man of genius."

It was during his residence in Philadelphia that Poe wrote his choicest stories. Among the masterpieces of this period are to be mentioned *The Fall of the House of Usher*, *Ligeia*, which he regarded as his best tale *The Descent into the Maelstrom*, *The Murders in the Rue Morgue*, and *The Mystery of Marie Roget*. The general character of his tales may be inferred from their titles. Poe delighted in the weird, fantastic, dismal, horrible. There is no warmth of human sympathy, no moral consciousness, no lessons of practical wisdom. His tales are the product of a morbid but powerful imagination. His style is in perfect keeping with his peculiar gifts. He had a highly developed artistic sense. By his air of perfect candor, his minuteness of detail, and his power of graphic description, he gains complete mastery over the soul, and leads us almost to believe the impossible. Within the limited range of his imagination (for he was by no means the universal genius he fancied himself to be) he is unsurpassed, perhaps, by any other American writer.

Poe's career had now reached its climax, and after a time began its rapid descent. In 1844 he moved to New York, where for a year or two his life did not differ materially from what it had been in Philadelphia. He continued to write his fantastic tales, for which he was poorly paid, and to do editorial work, by which he eked out a scanty livelihood. He was employed by N. P. Willis for a few months on the *Evening Mirror* as sub-editor and critic, and was regularly "at his desk from nine in the morning till the paper went to press."

It was in this paper, January 29, 1845, that his greatest poem, *The Raven*, was published with a flattering commendation by Willis. It laid hold of the popular fancy; and, copied throughout the length and breadth of the land, it met a reception never before accorded to an American poem. Abroad its success was scarcely less remarkable and decisive. "This vivid writing," wrote Mrs. Browning, "this power *which is felt*, has produced a sensation here in England. Some of my friends are taken by the fear of it, and some by the music. I hear of persons who are haunted by the ' Nevermore '; and an acquaintance of mine, who has the misfortune of possessing a bust of Pallas, cannot bear to look at it in the twilight."

In 1845 Poe was associated with the management of the *Broadway Journal*, which in a few months passed entirely into his hands. He had long desired to control a periodical of his own, and in Philadelphia had tried to establish a magazine. But, however brilliant as an editor, he was not a man of administrative ability; and in three months he was forced to suspend publication for want of means. Shortly afterward he published in Godey's *Lady's Book* a series of critical papers entitled *Literati of New York*. The papers, usually brief, are gossipy, interesting, sensational, with an occasional lapse into contemptuous and exasperating severity.

In the same year he published a tolerably complete edition of his poems in the revised form in which they now appear in his works. The volume contained nearly all the poems upon which his poetic fame justly rests. Among those that may be regarded as embodying his highest poetic achievement are *The Raven*, *Lenore*, *Ulalume*, *The Bells*, *Annabel Lee*, *The Haunted Palace*, *The Conqueror Worm*, *The City in the Sea*, *Eulalie*, and *Israfel*. Rarely has so large a fame rested on so small a number of poems, and rested so securely. His range of themes, it will be noticed, is very narrow. As in his tales, he dwells in a weird, fantastic, or desolate region — usually under the shadow of death. He conjures up unearthly landscapes as a setting for his gloomy and morbid fancies. In *The City in the Sea*, for example: —

> "There shrines and palaces and towers
> (Time-eaten towers that tremble not!)
> Resemble nothing that is ours.
> Around, by lifting winds forgot,
> Resignedly beneath the sky
> The melancholy waters lie."

He conformed his poetic efforts to his theory that a poem should be short. He maintained that the phrase "'a long poem' is simply a flat contradiction in terms." His strong artistic sense gave him a firm mastery over form. He constantly uses alliteration, assonance, repetition, and refrain. These artifices form an essential part of *The Raven*, *Lenore*, and *The Bells*. In his poems, as in his tales, Poe was less anxious to set forth an experience or a truth than to make an impression. His poetry aims at beauty in a purely artistic sense, unassociated with truth or morals. It is, for the most part, singularly vague, unsubstantial, and melodious. Some of his poems —and precisely those in which his genius finds its highest expression — defy complete analysis. *Ulalume*, for instance, remains obscure after the twentieth

perusal — its meaning lost in a haze of mist and
music.   Yet these poems, when read in a sympathetic mood, never fail of their effect.   They are
genuine creations; and, as a fitting expression of
certain mental states, they possess an indescribable
charm, something like the spell of the finest instru-
mental music.   There is no mistaking Poe's poetic
genius.   Though not the greatest, he is still the
most original, of our poets, and has fairly earned
the high esteem in which his gifts are held in
America and Europe.

During his stay in New York, Poe was often
present in the literary gatherings of the metropolis.
He was sometimes accompanied by his sweet, affec-
tionate, invalid wife, whom in her fourteenth year
he had married in Richmond.   According to Griswold, " His conversation was at times almost supra-
mortal in its eloquence.   His voice was modulated
with astonishing skill; and his large and variably
expressive eyes looked repose or shot fiery tumult
into theirs who listened, while his own face glowed,
or was changeless in pallor, as his imagination
quickened his blood or drew it back frozen to his
heart."   His writings are unstained by a single
immoral sentiment.

Toward the latter part of his sojourn in New York,
the hand of poverty and want pressed upon him
sorely.   The failing health of his wife, to whom
his tender devotion is beyond all praise, was a
source of deep and constant anxiety.   For a time
he became an object of charity — a humiliation that
was exceedingly galling to his delicately sensitive

nature. To a sympathetic friend, who lent her kindly aid in this time of need, we owe a graphic but pathetic picture of Poe's home shortly before the death of his almost angelic wife: "There was no clothing on the bed, which was only straw, but a snow-white counterpane and sheets. The weather was cold, and the sick lady had the dreadful chills that accompany the hectic fever of consumption. She lay on the straw bed, wrapped in her husband's great-coat, with a large tortoise-shell cat in her bosom. The wonderful cat seemed conscious of her great usefulness. The coat and the cat were the sufferer's only means of warmth, except as her husband held her hands, and her mother her feet." She died January 30, 1847.

After this event Poe was never entirely himself again. The immediate effect of his bereavement was complete physical and mental prostration, from which he recovered only with difficulty. His subsequent literary work deserves scarcely more than mere mention. His *Eureka*, an ambitious treatise, the immortality of which he confidently predicted, was a disappointment and failure. He tried lecturing, but with only moderate success. His correspondence at this time reveals a broken, hysterical, hopeless man. In his weakness, loneliness, and sorrow, he resorted to stimulants with increasing frequency. Their terrible work was soon done. On his return from a visit to Richmond, he stopped in Baltimore, where he died from the effects of drinking, October 7, 1849.

Thus ended the tragedy of his life. It is as

depressing as one of his own morbid, fantastic
tales.   His career leaves a painful sense of incom-
pleteness and loss.   With greater self-discipline,
how much more he might have accomplished for
himself and for others !   Gifted, self-willed, proud,
passionate, with meager moral sense, he forfeited
success by his perversity and his vices.   From his
own character and experience he drew the un-
healthy and pessimistic views to which he has
given expression in the maddening poem, *The
Conqueror Worm*.   And if there were not happier
and nobler lives, we might well say with him, as we
stand by his grave : —

> " Out — out are the lights — out all !
>   And, over each quivering form,
>   The curtain, a funeral pall,
>   Comes down with the rush of a storm,
>   And the angels, all pallid and wan,
>   Uprising, unveiling, affirm
>   That the play is the tragedy ' Man,'
>   And its hero the Conqueror Worm."

PAUL HAMILTON HAYNE.

CHAPTER III

THE poetry of Paul Hamilton Hayne is characterized by a singular delicacy of sentiment and
expression. There is an utter absence of what is
gross or commonplace. His poetry, as a whole,
carries with it an atmosphere of high-bred refinement. We recognize at once fineness of fiber and
of culture. It could not well be otherwise; for
the poet traced the line of his ancestors to the
cultured nobility of England, and, surrounded by
wealth, was brought up in the home of Southern
chivalry.

The aristocratic lineage of the Hayne family
was not reflected in its political feelings and affili-
ations in this country. They were not Tories;
on the contrary, from the colonial days down to
the Civil War they showed themselves stoutly
democratic. The Haynes were, in a measure, to
South Carolina what the Adamses and Quincys
were to Massachusetts. A chivalrous uncle of the
poet, Colonel Arthur P. Hayne, fought in three
wars, and afterwards entered the United States
Senate. Another uncle, Governor Robert Y.
Hayne, was a distinguished statesman, who did

not fear to cross swords with Webster in the most famous debate, perhaps, of our national history. The poet's father was a lieutenant in the United States navy, and died at sea when his gifted son was still an infant. These patriotic antecedents were not without influence on the life and writings of the poet.

In the existing biographical sketches of Hayne we find little or no mention of his mother. This neglect is undeserved. She was a cultured woman of good English and Scotch ancestry. It was her hand that had the chief fashioning of the young poet's mind and heart. She transmitted to him his poetic temperament ; and when his muse began its earliest flights, she encouraged him with appreciative words and ambitious hopes. Hayne's poems are full of autobiographic elements ; and in one, entitled *To My Mother*, he says : —

> " To thee my earliest verse I brought,
>   All wreathed in loves and roses,
> Some glowing boyish fancy, fraught
>   With tender May-wind closes ;
> *Thou* didst not taunt my fledgling song,
>   Nor view its flight with scorning :
> ' The bird,' thou saidst, ' grown fleet and strong,
>   Might yet outsoar the morning ! ' "

Paul Hamilton Hayne was born in Charleston, South Carolina, January 1, 1830. At that time Charleston was the literary center of the South. Among its wealthy and aristocratic circles there was a literary group of unusual gifts. Calhoun

and Legaré were there; and William Gilmore
Simms, a man of great versatility, gathered about
him a congenial literary circle, in which we find
Hayne and his scarcely less distinguished friend,
Henry Timrod.

Hayne was graduated with distinction from
Charleston College in 1850, receiving a prize for
superiority in English composition and elocution.
He then studied law; but, like many other authors
both North and South, the love of letters proved
too strong for the practice of his profession. His
literary bent, as with most of our gifted authors,
manifested itself early, and even in his college
days he became a devotee of the poetic muse.
The ardor of his devotion found expression in one
of his early poems, first called *Aspirations*, but in
his later works appearing under the title of *The
Will and the Wing:* —

" Yet would I rather in the outward state
    Of Song's immortal temple lay me down,
  A beggar basking by that radiant gate,
    Than bend beneath the haughtiest empire's crown.

" For sometimes, through the bars, my ravished eyes
    Have caught brief glimpses of a life divine,
  And seen a far, mysterious rapture rise
    Beyond the veil that guards the inmost shrine."

Hayne served his literary apprenticeship in connection with several periodicals. He was a favorite contributor to the *Southern Literary Messenger*,
for many years published in Richmond, Virginia,

and deservedly ranking as the best monthly issued in the South before the Civil War. He was one of the editors of the *Southern Literary Gazette*, a weekly published in his native city. Afterwards, as a result of a plan devised at one of Simms's literary dinners, *Russell's Magazine*, with Hayne as editor, was established, to use the language of the first number, as "another depository for Southern genius, and a new incentive, as we hope, for its active exercise." It was a monthly of high excellence for the time; but for lack of adequate support it suspended publication after an honorable career of two years.

An article in *Russell's Magazine* for August, 1857, elaborately discusses the ante-bellum discouragements to authorship in the South. Indifference, ignorance, and prejudice, the article asserted, were encountered on every hand. "It may happen to be only a volume of noble poetry, full of those universal thoughts and feelings which speak, not to a particular people, but to all mankind. It is censured, at the South, as not sufficiently Southern in spirit, while at the North it is pronounced a very fair specimen of Southern commonplace. Both North and South agree with one mind to condemn the author and forget his book."

Hayne's critical work as editor of *Russell's Magazine* is worthy of note. In manly independence of judgment, though not in ferocity of style, he resembled Poe. He prided himself on conscientious loyalty to literary art. He disclaimed all sympathy with that sectional spirit which has sometimes lauded a work merely for geographical reasons; and in the critical reviews of his magazine he did not hesitate to point out and censure crudeness in Southern writers. But, at the same time, it was a more pleasing task to his generous nature to recognize and praise artistic excellence wherever he found it.

As a critic Hayne was, perhaps, severest to himself. His poetic standards were high. In his maturer years he blamed the precipitancy with which, as a youth, he had rushed into print. There is an interesting marginal note, as his son tells us, in a copy of his first volume of verse, in which *The Cataract* is pronounced "the poorest piece in the volume. Boyish and bombastic! Should have been whipped for publishing it!" It is needless to say that the piece does not appear in his *Complete Poems*. This severity of self-criticism, which exacted sincerity of utterance, has imparted a rare average excellence to his work.

In 1852 he married Miss Mary Middleton Michel, of Charleston, the daughter of a distinguished French physician. Rarely has a union been more happy. In the days of his prosperity she was an inspiration; and in the long years of poverty and sickness that came later she was his comfort and stay. In his poem, *The Bonny Brown Hand*, there is a reflection of the love that glorified the toil and ills of this later period: —

" Oh, drearily, how drearily, the sombre eve comes
        down !
    And wearily, how wearily, the seaboard breezes
        blow !
    But place your little hand in mine — so dainty, yet so
        brown !
        For household toil hath worn away its rosy-tinted
            snow ;
                But I fold it, wife, the nearer,
                And I feel, my love, 'tis dearer
                Than all dear things of earth,
                As I watch the pensive gloaming,
                And my wild thoughts cease from roaming,
    And birdlike furl their pinions close beside our peace-
        ful hearth ;
        Then rest your little hand in mine, while twilight
            shimmers down,
        That little hand, that fervent hand, that hand of
            bonny brown —
    The hand that holds an honest heart, and rules a
        happy hearth."

Two small volumes of Hayne's poetry appeared
before the Civil War from the press of Ticknor &
Co., Boston.   They were made up chiefly of pieces
contributed to the *Southern Literary Messenger*,
Russsell's Magazine, and other periodicals in the
South.   The first volume appeared in 1855, and
the second in 1859.   These volumes were well
worthy of the favorable reception they met with,
and encouraged the poet to dedicate himself more
fully to his art.   In the fullness of this dedica-
tion, he reminds us of Longfellow, Tennyson,

and Wordsworth, all of whom he admired and loved.

Few first volumes of greater excellence have ever appeared in this country. The judicious critic was at once able to recognize the presence of a genuine singer. The poet rises above the obvious imitation that was a common vice among Southern singers before the Civil War. We may indeed perceive the influence of Tennyson in the delicacy of the craftsmanship, and the influence of Wordsworth in the deep and sympathetic treatment of Nature; but Hayne's study of these great bards had been transmuted into poetic culture, and is reflected only in the superior quality of his work. There is no case of conscious or obvious imitation.

The volume of 1859, which bears the title *Avolio and Other Poems*, exhibits the poet's fondness for the sonnet and his admirable skill in its use. Throughout his subsequent poetical career, he frequently chose the sonnet as the medium for expressing his choicest thought. It is hardly too much to claim that Hayne is the prince of American sonneteers. The late Maurice Thompson said that he could pick out twenty of Hayne's sonnets equal to almost any others in our language. In the following sonnet, which is quoted by way of illustration, the poet gives us the key to a large part of his work. He was a worshiper of beauty; and the singleness of this devotion gives him his distinctive place in our poetic annals.

" Pent in this common sphere of sensual shows,
   I pine for beauty ; beauty of fresh mien,
     And gentle utterance, and the charm serene,
Wherewith the hue of mystic dreamland glows ;
I pine for lulling music, the repose
   Of low-voiced waters, in some realm between
   The perfect Adenne, and this clouded scene
Of love's sad loss, and passion's mournful throes ;
A pleasant country, girt with twilight calm,
   In whose fair heaven a moon of shadowy round
     Wades through a fading fall of sunset rain ;
Where drooping lotos-flowers, distilling balm,
   Gleam by the drowsy streamlets sleep hath crown'd,
     While Care forgets to sigh, and Peace hath bal-
       samed pain."

The great civil conflict of '61–'65 naturally stirred the poet's heart. He was a patriotic son of the South. On the breaking out of hostilities, he became a member of Governor Pickens's staff, and was stationed for a time in Fort Sumter ; but after a brief service he was forced to resign on account of failing health. His principal service to the Southern cause was rendered in his martial songs, which breathe a lofty, patriotic spirit. They are remarkable at once for their dignity of manner and refinement of utterance. There is an entire absence of the fierceness that is to be found in some of Whittier's and Timrod's sectional lyrics. Hayne lacked the fierce energy of a great re-former or partisan leader. But nowhere else do we find a heart more sensitive to grandeur of achievement or pathos of incident. He recognized

the unsurpassed heroism of sentiment and achievement displayed in the war; and in an admirable
sonnet, he exclaims:—

" Ah, foolish souls and false ! who loudly cried
    ' True chivalry no longer breathes in time.'
    Look round us now ; how wondrous, how sublime
The heroic lives we witness ; far and wide
Stern vows by sterner deeds are justified ;
    Self-abnegation, calmness, courage, power,
    Sway, with a rule august, our stormy hour,
Wherein the loftiest hearts have wrought and died —
Wrought grandly, and died smiling.   Thus, O God,
    From tears, and blood, and anguish, thou hast
        brought
    The ennobling act, the faith-sustaining thought —
Till, in the marvelous present, one may see
A mighty stage, by knights and patriots trod,
Who had not shunned earth's haughtiest chivalry."

The war brought the poet disaster. His beautiful home and the library he has celebrated in a
noble sonnet were destroyed in the bombardment
of Charleston.   The family silver, which had been
stored in Columbia for safe-keeping, was lost in
Sherman's famous " march to the sea."   His
native state was in desolation ; his friends, warm
and true with the fidelity which a common disaster
brings, were generally as destitute and helpless
as himself.   Under these disheartening circumstances, rendered still more gloomy by the ruthless
deeds of reconstruction, he withdrew to the pine
barrens of Georgia, where, eighteen miles from

Augusta, he built a very plain and humble cottage. He christened it Copse Hill; and it was here, on a desk fashioned out of a workbench left by the carpenters, that many of his choicest pieces, reflecting credit on American letters, and earning for him a high place among American poets, were written.

This modest home, which from its steep hillside —

"Catches morn's earliest and eve's latest glow," —

the poet has commemorated in a sonnet, which gives us a glimpse of the quiet, rural scenes that were dear to his heart: —

"Here, far from worldly strife, and pompous show,
    The peaceful seasons glide serenely by,
    Fulfill their missions, and as calmly die,
As waves on quiet shores when winds are low.
Fields, lonely paths, the one small glimmering rill
    That twinkles like a wood-fay's mirthful eye,
    Under moist bay leaves, clouds fantastical
That float and change at the light breeze's will, —
    To me, thus lapped in sylvan luxury,
    Are more than death of kings, or empires' fall."

His son, Mr. W. H. Hayne, has thrown an interesting light upon the poet's methods of composition. Physical movement seemed favorable to his poetic faculty; and many of his pieces were composed as he paced to and fro in his study, or walked with stooping shoulders beneath the trees surrounding Copse Hill. He was not mechanical or systematic in his poetic work, but followed the impulse of inspiration. "The poetic impulse," his son tells us, "frequently came to him so spontaneously as to demand immediate utterance, and he would turn to the fly leaf of the book in hand or on a neighboring shelf, and his pencil would soon record the lines, or fragments of lines, that claimed release from his brain. The labor of revision usually followed, — sometimes promptly, but not infrequently after the fervor of conception had passed away." The painstaking care with which the revising was done is revealed in the artistic finish of almost every poem.

Hayne's life at this time was truly heroic. With uncomplaining fortitude he met the hardships of poverty and bore the increasing ills of failing health. He never lost hope and courage. He lived the poetry that he sang : —

> " Still smiles the brave soul, undivorced from hope ;
>   And, with unwavering eye and warrior mien,
>   Walks in the shadow dauntless and serene,
> To test, through hostile years, the utmost scope
>   Of man's endurance — constant to essay
>   All heights of patience free to feet of clay."

And in the end he was not disappointed. Gradually his genius gained general recognition. The leading magazines of the country were opened to him; and, as Stedman remarks, "his people regarded him with a tenderness which, if a com-

mensurate largess had been added, would have
made him feel less solitary among his pines."

In 1872 a volume of *Legends and Lyrics* was
issued by Lippincott & Co. It shows the poet's
genius in the full power of maturity. His legends
are admirably told, and *Aëthra* is a gem of its
kind. But the richness of Hayne's imagination
was better suited to lyric than to narrative or dra-
matic poetry. The latter, indeed, abounds in rare
beauty of thought and expression; but somehow
this luxuriance seems to retard or obscure the movement. The lyric pieces of this volume are full of
self-revelation, autobiography, and Southern landscape. Hayne was not an apostle of the strenuous
life; he preferred to dream among the beauties or
sublimities of Nature. Thus, in *Dolce far Niente*,
he says : —

> " Let the world roll blindly on !
> Give me shadow, give me sun,
> And a perfumed eve as this is :
> Let me lie
> Dreamfully,
> Where the last quick sunbeams shiver
> Spears of light athwart the river,
> And a breeze, which seems the sigh
> Of a fairy floating by,
> Coyly kisses
> Tender leaf and feathered grasses ;
> Yet so soft its breathing passes,
> These tall ferns, just glimmering o'er me,
> Blending goldenly before me,
> Hardly quiver ! "

The well-known friendship existing between Hayne and his brother poet Timrod was a beautiful one. As schoolboys they had encouraged each other in poetic efforts. As editor of *Russell's Magazine*, Hayne had welcomed and praised Timrod's contributions. For the edition of Timrod's poems published in 1873, Hayne prepared a generous and beautiful memoir, in which he quoted the opinion of some Northern writers who assigned the highest place to his friend among the poets of the South. In the *Legends and Lyrics* there is a fine poem, *Under the Pine*, commemorative of Timrod's visit to Copse Hill shortly before his death : —

> " O Tree ! against thy mighty trunk he laid
>   His weary head ; thy shade
> Stole o'er him like the first cool spell of sleep:
>   It brought a peace *so* deep,
> The unquiet passion died from out his eyes,
>   As lightnings from stilled skies.

> " And in that calm he loved to rest, and hear
>   The soft wind-angels, clear
> And sweet, among the uppermost branches sighing :
>   Voices he heard replying
> (Or so he dreamed) far up the mystic height,
>   And pinions rustling light."

As illustrating his rich fancy and graphic power of diction, a few stanzas are given from *Cloud Pictures*. They are not unworthy of Tennyson in his happiest moments.

" At calm length I lie
Fronting the broad blue spaces of the sky,
Covered with cloud-groups, softly journeying by :

" An hundred shapes, fantastic, beauteous, strange,
Are theirs, as o'er yon airy waves they range
At the wind's will, from marvelous change to change :

" Castles, with guarded roof, and turret tall,
Great sloping archway, and majestic wall,
Sapped by the breezes to their noiseless fall !

" Pagodas vague ! above whose towers outstream
Banners that wave with motions of a dream —
Rising or drooping in the noontide gleam ;

" Gray lines of Orient pilgrims : a gaunt band
On famished camels, o'er the desert sand
Plodding towards their prophet's Holy Land ;

" Mid-ocean, — and a shoal of whales at play,
Lifting their monstrous frontlets to the day,
Through rainbow arches of sun-smitten spray ;

" Followed by splintered icebergs, vast and lone,
Set in swift currents of some arctic zone,
Like fragments of a Titan world o'erthrown."

In 1882 a complete edition of Hayne's poems
was published by D. Lothrop & Co. Except a
few poems written after that date and still uncollected, this edition contains his later productions,
in which we discover an increasing seriousness,
richness, and depth. The general range of subjects, as in his earlier volumes, is limited to his

Southern environment and individual experience.
This limitation is the severest charge that can be
brought against his poetry, but, at the same time,
it is an evidence of his sincerity and truth. He
did not aspire, as did some of his great Northern
contemporaries, to the office of moralist, philosopher, or reformer. He was content to dwell in the
quiet realm of beauty as it appears, to use the
words of Margaret J. Preston, in the "aromatic
freshness of the woods, the swaying incense of
the cathedral-like isles of pines, the sough of dying
summer winds, the glint of lonely pools, and the
brooding notes of leaf-hidden mocking-birds."
But the beauty and pathos of human life were
not forgotten ; and now and then he touched upon
the great spiritual truths on which the splendid
heroism of his life was built. For delicacy of feeling and perfection of form, his meditative and
religious poems deserve to rank among the best
in our language. They contain what is so often
lacking in poetry of this class, genuine poetic feeling and artistic expression.

The steps of death approached gradually ; for,
like two other great poets of the South, Timrod
and Lanier, he was not physically strong. Though
sustained through his declining years by " the ulti-
mate trust " —

"That love and mercy, Father, still are thine," —

he felt a pathetic desire to linger awhile in the
love of his tender, patient, helpful wife : —

" A little while I fain would linger here ;
  Behold ! who knows what soul-dividing bars
  Earth's faithful loves may part in other stars ?
Nor can love deem the face of death is fair :
A little while I still would linger here."

Paul Hamilton Hayne passed away July 6, 1886. As already brought out in the course of this sketch, he was not only a gifted singer, but also a noble man. His extraordinary poetic gifts have not yet been fully recognized. Less gifted singers have been placed above him. No biography has been written to record with fond minuteness the story of his admirable life and achievement. His writings in prose, and a few of his choicest lyrics, still remain unpublished. Let us hope that this reproach to Southern letters may soon be removed, and that this laureate of the South may yet come to the full inheritance of fame to which the children of genius are inalienably entitled.

CHAPTER IV

HENRY TIMROD

In some respects there is a striking similarity in the lives of the three Southern poets, Hayne, Timrod, and Lanier. They were alike victims of misfortune, and in their greatest tribulations they exhibited the same heroic patience and fortitude.

> "They knew alike what suffering starts
>   From fettering need and ceaseless pain;
> But still with brave and cheerful hearts,
> Whose message hope and joy imparts,
>   They sang their deathless strain."

The fate of Timrod was the saddest of them all. Gifted with uncommon genius, he never saw its full fruitage; and over and over again, when some precious hope seemed about to be realized, it was cruelly dashed to the ground. There is, perhaps, no sadder story in the annals of literature.

Henry Timrod was born in Charleston, South Carolina, December 28, 1829. He was older than his friend Hayne by twenty-three days. The law of heredity seems to find exemplification in his genius. The Timrods, a family of German descent, were long identified with the history of South

HENRY TIMROD.

Carolina. The poet's grandfather belonged to the German Fusiliers of Charleston, a volunteer company organized in 1775, after the battle of Lexington, for the defense of the American colonies. In the Seminole War, the poet's father, Captain William Henry Timrod, commanded the German Fusiliers in Florida. He was a gifted man, whose talents attracted an admiring circle of friends. "By the simple mastery of genius," says Hayne, "he gained no trifling influence among the highest intellectual and social circles of a city noted at that period for aristocratic exclusiveness."

Timrod's father was not only an eloquent talker, but also a poet. A strong intellect was associated with delicate feelings. He had the gift of musical utterance; and the following verses from his poem, *To Time — the Old Traveler*, were pronounced by Washington Irving equal to any lyric written by Tom Moore: —

> " They slander thee, Old Traveler,
>   Who say that thy delight
> Is to scatter ruin far and wide,
>   In thy wantonness of might:
> For not a leaf that falleth
>   Before thy restless wings,
> But in thy flight, thou changest it
>   To a thousand brighter things.
>
>   *   *   *   *   *
>
> " 'Tis true thy progress layeth
>   Full many a loved one low,
> And for the brave and beautiful
>   Thou hast caused our tears to flow;

But always near the couch of death
  Nor thou, nor we can stay;
And the breath of thy departing wings
  Dries all our tears away!"

On his mother's side the poet was scarcely less fortunate in his parentage. She was as beautiful in form and face as in character. From her more than from his father the poet derived his love of Nature. She delighted in flowers and trees and stars; she caught the glintings of the sunshine through the leaves; she felt a thrill of joy at the music of singing birds and of murmuring waters. With admirable maternal tenderness she taught her children to discern and appreciate the lovely sights and sounds of nature.

Timrod received his early education in a Charleston school, where he sat next to Hayne. He was an ambitious boy, insatiable in his desire for knowledge; at the same time, he was fond of outdoor sports, and enjoyed the respect and confidence of his companions. His poetic activity dates from this period. "I well remember," says Hayne, "the exultation with which he showed me one morning his earliest consecutive attempt at verse-making. Our down-East schoolmaster, however, could boast of no turn for sentiment, and having remarked us hobnobbing, meanly assaulted us in the rear, effectually quenching for the time all æsthetic enthusiasm."

When sixteen or seventeen years of age he entered the University of Georgia. He was cramped for lack of means; sickness interfered with his studies, and at length he was forced to leave the university without his degree. But his interrupted course was not in vain. His fondness for literature led him, not only to an intelligent study of Virgil, Horace, and Catullus, but also to an unusual acquaintance with the leading poets of England. His pen was not inactive, and some of his college verse, published over a fictitious signature in a Charleston paper, attracted local attention.

After leaving college Timrod returned to Charleston, and entered upon the study of law in the office of the Hon. J. L. Petigru. But the law was not adapted to his tastes and talents, and, like Hayne, he early abandoned it to devote himself to literature. He was timid and retiring in disposition. "His walk was quick and nervous," says Dr. J. Dickson Bruns, "with an energy in it that betokened decision of character, but ill sustained by the stammering speech; for in society he was the shyest and most undemonstrative of men. To a single friend whom he trusted, he would pour out his inmost heart; but let two or three be gathered together, above all, introduce a stranger, and he instantly became a quiet, unobtrusive listener, though never a moody or uncongenial one."

He aspired to a college professorship, for which he made diligent preparation in the classics; but in spite of his native abilities and excellent attainments, he never secured this object of his ambition. Leaving Charleston, he became a tutor in private families; but on holiday occasions he was accus-

tomed to return to the city, where he was cordially
welcomed by his friends. Among these was William
Gilmore Simms, a sort of Mæcenas to aspiring
genius, who gathered about him the younger
literary men of his acquaintance. At the little
dinners he was accustomed to give, no one manifested a keener enjoyment than Timrod, when, in
the words of Hayne : —

> " Around the social board
>   The impetuous flood tide poured
> Of curbless mirth, and keen sparkling jest
> Vanished like wine-foam on its golden crest."

During all these years of toil and waiting the
poetic muse was not idle. Under the pseudonym
" Aglaus," the name of a minor pastoral poet of
Greece, he became a frequent and favorite contributor to the *Southern Literary Messenger* of
Richmond, Virginia. Later he became one of the
principal contributors, both in prose and poetry, to
Russell's Magazine in Charleston. It was in these
periodicals that the foundation of his fame was
laid.

Timrod's first volume of poetry, made up of
pieces taken chiefly from these magazines, appeared in 1860, from the press of Ticknor & Fields,
Boston. It was Hayne's judgment that "a better
first volume of the kind has seldom appeared anywhere." It contains most of the pieces found in
subsequent editions of his works. Here and there,
both North and South, a discerning critic recog-

nized in the poet "a lively, delicate fancy, and a graceful beauty of expression." But, upon the whole, the book attracted little attention — a fact that came to the poet as a deep disappointment. In the words of Dr. Bruns, who was familiar with the circumstances of the poet, "success was to him a bitter need, for not his *living* merely, but his *life* was staked upon it."

When this volume appeared, Timrod was more than a poetic tyro. Apart from native inspiration, in which he was surpassed by few of his contemporaries, he had reflected profoundly on his art, and nursed his genius on the masterpieces of English song. In addition to Shakespeare he had carefully pondered Milton, Wordsworth, and Tennyson. From Wordsworth especially he learned to appreciate the poetry of common things, and to discern the mystic presence of that spirit, —

"Whose dwelling is the light of setting suns,
And the round ocean, and the living air,
And the blue sky, and in the mind of man."

Timrod, like Poe, formulated a theory of poetry which it is interesting to study, as it throws light on his own work. It reveals to us the ideal at which he aimed. In a famous essay Poe made beauty the sole realm and end of poetry. To Timrod belongs the credit of setting forth a larger and juster conception of the poetic art. To beauty he adds *power* and *truth* as legitimate sources of poetry. "I think," he says, "when we recall the many and

varied sources of poetry, we must, perforce, confess that it is wholly impossible to reduce them all
to the simple element of beauty. Two other elements, at least, must be added, and these are power,
when it is developed in some noble shape, and truth,
whether abstract or not, when it affects the common
heart of mankind."

Timrod regarded a poem as a work of art. He
justly held that a poem should have "one purpose,
and that the materials of which it is composed
should be so selected and arranged as to help en-
force it." He distinguished between the moment
of inspiration, "when the great thought strikes for
the first time along the brain and flushes the cheek
with the sudden revelation of beauty or grandeur,
and the hour of patient, elaborate execution." Accordingly he quoted with approval the lines of
Matthew Arnold : —

> " We cannot kindle when we will
>   The fire that in the heart resides ;
> The spirit bloweth and is still ;
>   In mystery our soul abides ;
> But tasks in hours of insight willed,
> May be through hours of gloom fulfilled."

Timrod's poetry is characterized by clearness,
simplicity, and force. He was not a mystic; his
thoughts and emotions are not obscured in voluble
melody. To him poetry is more than rhythmic harmony. Beneath his delicate imagery and rhyth-
mical sweetness are poured treasures of thought
and truth. In diction he belongs to the school of

Wordsworth; his language is not strained or far-fetched, but such as is natural to cultured men in a state of emotion. " Poetry," he says in an early volume of *Russell's Magazine*, " does not deal in abstractions. However abstract be his thought, the poet is compelled, by his passion-fused imagination, to give it life, form, or color. Hence the necessity of employing the *sensuous or concrete* words of the language, and hence the exclusion of long words, which in English are nearly all purely and austerely *abstract*, from the poetic vocabulary."

He defends the use of the sonnet, in which, like Hayne, he excelled. He admits that the sonnet is artificial in structure; but, as already pointed out, he distinguishes the moment of inspiration, from the subsequent labor of composition. In the act of writing, the poet passes into the artist. And " the very restriction so much complained of in the sonnet," he says, " the artist knows to be an advantage. It forces him to condensation." His sonnets are characterized by a rare lucidity of thought and expression.

The principal piece in Timrod's first volume, to which we now return, and the longest poem he ever wrote, is entitled *A Vision of Poesy*. In the experience of the imaginative hero, who seems an idealized portrait of the poet himself, we find an almost unequaled presentation of the nature and uses of poetry. The spirit of Poesy, "the angel of the earth," thus explains her lofty mission : —

" And ever since that immemorial hour
 When the glad morning stars together sung,
My task hath been, beneath a mightier Power,
 To keep the world forever fresh and young ;
I give it not its fruitage and its green,
But clothe it with a glory all unseen."

And what are the objects on which this angel
of Poesy loves to dwell ? Truth, freedom, passion,
she answers, and —

" All lovely things, and gentle — the sweet laugh
 Of children, girlhood's kiss, and friendship's clasp,
The boy that sporteth with the old man's staff,
 The baby, and the breast its fingers grasp —
All that exalts the grounds of happiness,
All griefs that hallow, and all joys that bless,

" To me are sacred ; at my holy shrine
 Love breathes its latest dreams, its earliest hints ;
I turn life's tasteless waters into wine,
 And flush them through and through with purple
  tints.
Wherever earth is fair, and heaven looks down,
I rear my altars, and I wear my crown."

Many of the poems in this first volume are worthy
of note, as revealing some phase of the poet's ver-
satile gifts — delicate fancy, simplicity and truth,
lucid force, or finished art. *The Lily Confidante*,
is a light, lilting fancy, the moral of which is : —

" Love's the lover's only magic,
 Truth the very subtlest art ;
Love that feigns, and lips that flatter,
 Win no modest heart."

The Past was first published in the *Southern Literary Messenger*, and afterwards went the rounds of the press. It teaches the important truth that we are the sum of all we have lived through. The past forms the atmosphere which we breathe to-day; it is —

" A shadowy land, where joy and sorrow kiss,
    Each still to each corrective and relief,
Where dim delights are brightened into bliss
    And nothing wholly perishes but grief.

" Ah me ! — not dies — no more than spirit dies ;
    But in a change like death is clothed with wings ;
A serious angel, with entrancèd eyes,
    Looking to far-off and celestial things."

Timrod possessed an ardent spirit that was stirred to its depths by the Civil War. His martial songs, with their fierce intensity, better voiced the feelings of the South at that time than those of Hayne or any other Southern singer. In his *Ethnogenesis* — the birth of a nation — he celebrates in a lofty strain the rise of the Confederacy, of which he cherished large and generous hopes : —

                            " The type
Whereby we shall be known in every land
Is that vast gulf which lips our Southern strand,
And through the cold, untempered ocean pours
Its genial streams, that far off Arctic shores
May sometimes catch upon the softened breeze
Strange tropic warmth and hints of summer seas."

But his most stirring lyrics are *Carolina* and *A Cry to Arms*, which in the exciting days of '61 deeply moved the Southern heart, but which to-day serve as melancholy mementos of a long-past sectional bitterness. Of the vigorous lines of the former, Hayne says in an interesting autobiographic touch, "I read them first, and was thrilled by their power and pathos, upon a stormy March evening in Fort Sumter! Walking along the battlements, under the red lights of a tempestuous sunset, the wind steadily and loudly blowing from off the bar across the tossing and moaning waste of waters, driven inland; with scores of gulls and white sea-birds flying and shrieking round me, — those wild voices of Nature mingled strangely with the rhythmic roll and beat of the poet's impassioned music. The very spirit, or dark genius, of the troubled scene appeared to take up, and to repeat such verses as : —

> " ' I hear a murmur as of waves
>   That grope their way through sunless caves,
>   Like bodies struggling in their graves,
> > Carolina !

> " ' And now it deepens ; slow and grand
>   It swells, as rolling to the land,
>   An ocean broke upon the strand,
> > Carolina ! ' "

These impassioned war lyrics brought the poet speedy popularity. For a time his hopes were lifted up to a roseate future. In 1862 some of his influential friends formed the project of bringing out a handsome edition of his poems in London. The war correspondent of the *London Illustrated News*, himself an artist, volunteered to furnish original illustrations. The scheme, at which the poet was elated, promised at once bread and fame. But, as in so many other instances, he was doomed to bitter disappointment. The increasing stress of the great conflict absorbed the energies of the South; and the promising plan, notwithstanding the poet's popularity, was buried beneath the noise and tumult of battle.

Disqualified by feeble health from serving in the ranks, Timrod, shortly after the battle of Shiloh, went to Tennessee as the war correspondent of the *Charleston Mercury*. To his retiring and sympathetic nature the scenes of war were painful. "One can scarcely conceive," says Dr. Bruns, "of a situation more hopelessly wretched than that of a mere child in the world's ways suddenly flung down into the heart of that strong retreat, and tossed like a straw on the crest of those refluent waves, from which he escaped as by a miracle."

In 1863 he went to Columbia as associate editor of the *South Carolinian*. He was scarcely less happy and vigorous in prose than in verse. A period of prosperity seemed at last to be dawning; and, in the cheerful prospect, he ventured to marry Miss Kate Goodwin of Charleston, "Katie, the fair Saxon," whom he had long loved and of whom he had sung in one of his longest and sweetest poems. But his happiness was of brief duration.

In a twelvemonth the army of General Sherman entered Columbia, demolished his office, and sent him adrift as a helpless fugitive.

The close of the war found him a ruined man; he was almost destitute of property and broken in health. He was obliged to sell some of his household furniture to keep his family in bread. "We have," he says, in a sadly playful letter to Hayne at this period, " we have — let me see! — yes, we have eaten two silver pitchers, one or two dozen silver forks, several sofas, innumerable chairs, and a huge — bedstead!" He could find no paying market for his poems in the impoverished South; and in the North political feeling was still too strong to give him access to the magazines there. The only employment he could find was some clerical work for a season in the governor's office, where he sometimes toiled far beyond his strength. In this time of discouragement and need, the gloom of which was never lifted, he pathetically wrote to Hayne : "I would consign every line of my verse to eternal oblivion for *one hundred dollars in hand.*"

In 1867 his physicians recommended a change of air; and accordingly he spent a month with his lifelong friend Hayne at Copse Hill. It was the one rift in the clouds before the fall of night. There is a pathetic beauty in the fellowship of the two poets during these brief weeks, when, with spirits often attuned to high thought and feeling, they roamed together among the pines or sat beneath the stars. "We would rest on the hillsides," says Hayne, " in the swaying golden shadows, watching together the Titanic masses of snow-white clouds which floated slowly and vaguely through the sky, suggesting by their form, whiteness, and serene motion, despite the season, flotillas of icebergs upon Arctic seas. Like lazzaroni we basked in the quiet noons, sunk in the depths of reverie, or perhaps of yet more 'charmed sleep.' Or we smoked, conversing lazily between the puffs, —

' Next to some pine whose antique roots just peeped
From out the crumbling bases of the sand.' "

Timrod survived but a few weeks after his return to Columbia. The circumstances of his death were most pathetic. Though sustained by Christian hopes, he still longed to live a season with the dear ones about him. When, after a period of intense agony that preceded his dissolution, his sister murmured to him, "You will soon be at rest *now*," he replied, with touching pathos, "Yes, my sister, *but love is sweeter than rest*." He died October 7, 1867, and was laid to rest in Trinity churchyard, where his grave long remained unmarked.

Two principal editions of his works have been published: the first in 1873, with an admirable memoir by Hayne; the second in 1899, under the auspices of the Timrod Memorial Association of South Carolina. A number of his poems and his prose writings still remain uncollected; and there is yet no biography that fully records the story of his life. This fact is not a credit to Southern letters, for, as we have seen, Timrod was a poet of more than commonplace ability and achievement.

For the most part, his themes were drawn from the ordinary scenes and incidents of life. He was not ambitious of lofty subjects, remote from the hearts and homes of men. He placed sincerity above grandeur; he preferred love to admiration. He was always pure, brave, and true; and, as he sang: —

" The brightest stars are nearest to the earth,
And we may track the mighty sun above,
Even by the shadow of a slender flower.
Always, O bard, humility is power!
And thou mayest draw from matters of the hearth
Truths wide as nations, and as deep as love."

CHAPTER V

SIDNEY LANIER

LANIER'S genius was predominantly musical. He descended from a musical ancestry, which included in its line a "master of the king's music" at the court of James I. His musical gifts manifested themselves in early childhood. Without further instruction in music than a knowledge of the notes, which he learned from his mother, he was able to play, almost by intuition, the flute, guitar, violin, piano, and organ. He organized his boyish playmates into an amateur minstrel band; and when in early manhood he began to confide his most intimate thoughts to a notebook, he wrote, "The prime inclination — that is, natural bent (which I have checked, though) — of my nature is to music, and for that I have the greatest talent; indeed, not boasting, for God gave it me, I have an extraordinary musical talent, and feel it within me plainly that I could rise as high as any composer."

This early bent and passion for music never left him. His thought continually turned to the subject of music, and in the silences of his soul he frequently heard wonderful melodies. In his novel, *Tiger Lilies*, he lauds music in a rapturous

SIDNEY LANIER.

strain : " Since in all holy worship, in all conditions of life, in all domestic, social, religious, political, and lonely individual doings ; in all passions, in all countries, earthly or heavenly ; in all stages of civilization, of time, or of eternity ; since, I say, in all these, music is always present to utter the shallowest or the deepest thoughts of man or spirit — let us cease to call music a fine art, to class it with delicate pastry cookery and confectionery, and to fear to make too much of it lest it should make us sick." At a later period, while seeking to regain his health by a sojourn in Texas, he wrote to his wife: "All day my soul hath been cutting swiftly into the great space of the subtle, unspeakable deep, driven by wind after wind of heavenly melody. The very inner spirit and essence of all wind-songs, bird-songs, passion-songs, folk-songs, country-songs, sex-songs, soul-songs, and body-songs, hath blown upon me in quick gusts like the breath of passion, and sailed me into a sea of vast dreams, whereof each wave is at once a vision and a melody."

This predominance of music in the genius of Lanier is at once the source of his strength and of his weakness in poetry. In his poems, and in his work entitled *The Science of English Verse*, it is the musical element of poetry upon which the principal emphasis is laid. This fact makes him the successor of Poe in American letters. Both in theory and in practice Lanier has, as we shall see, achieved admirable results. But, after all, the musical element of poetry is of minor importance.

It is a means, and not an end. No jingle of sound can replace the delicacy of fancy, nobleness of sentiment and energy of thought that constitute what we may call the soul of poetry. Rhapsody is not the highest form of poetic achievement. In its noblest forms poetry is the medium through which great souls, like Homer, Virgil, Shakespeare, Milton, Tennyson, give to the world, with classic self-restraint, the fruitage of their highest thought and emotion.

The life of Lanier was a tragedy. While lighted here and there with a fleeting joy, its prevailing tone was one of sadness. The heroic courage with which he met disease and poverty impart to his life an inspiring grandeur. He was born at Macon, Georgia, February 3, 1842. His sensitive spirit early responded to the beauties of Nature; and in his hunting and fishing trips, in which he was usually accompanied by his younger brother Clifford, he caught something of the varied beauties of marsh, wood, and sky, which were afterwards to be so admirably woven into his poems. He early showed a fondness for books, and in the well-stored shelves of his father's library he found ample opportunity to gratify his taste for reading. His literary tastes were doubtless formed on the old English classics — Shakespeare, Milton, Pope, Addison — which formed a part of every Southern gentleman's library.

At the age of fifteen he entered the Sophomore class of Oglethorpe College, near Milledgeville, an institution that did not have sufficient vitality to

survive the Civil War. He did not think very
highly of the course of instruction, and found his
chief delight, as perhaps the best part of his culture, in the congenial circle of friends he gathered
around him. The evenings he spent with them
were frequently devoted to literature and music.
A classmate, Mr. T. F. Newell, gives us a vivid
picture of these social features of his college life.
" I can recall," he says, " my association with
him with sweetest pleasure, especially those Attic
nights, for they are among the dearest and tenderest recollections of my life, when with a few chosen
companions we would read from some treasured
volume, it may have been Tennyson, or Carlyle,
or Christopher North's *Noctes Ambrosianæ*, or
we would make the hours vocal with music and
song; those happy nights, which were veritable
refections bf the gods, and which will be remembered with no other regret than that they will nevermore return. On such occasions I have seen him
walk up and down the room and with his flute ex-
temporize the sweetest music ever vouchsafed to
mortal ear. At such times it would seem as if his
soul were in a trance, and could only find existence,
expression, in the ecstasy of tone, that would catch
our souls with his into the very seventh heaven of
harmony."

Lanier was a diligent student, and easily stood
among the first of his classes, particularly in mathematics. His reading took a wide range. In addition to the leading authors of the nineteenth century,
he showed a fondness for what was old and quaint

in our literature. He delighted in Burton's *Anatomy of Melancholy* and in the works of "the poet-preacher," Jeremy Taylor. At this time, too, his thoughtful nature turned to the serious problem of his life work. He eagerly questioned his capabilities as preliminary, to use his own words, "to ascertaining God's will with reference to himself." As already learned from his notebook, he early recognized his extraordinary gifts in music. But his ambition aimed at more than a musician's career, for it seemed to him, as he said, that there were greater things that he might do.

His ability and scholarship made a favorable impression on the college authorities, and immediately after his graduation he was elected to a tutorship. From this position, so congenial to his scholarly tastes, he was called, after six months, by the outbreak of the Civil War. In his boyhood he had shown a martial spirit. With his younger brother he joined the Macon Volunteers, and soon saw heavy service in Virginia. He took part in the battles of Seven Pines, Drewry's Bluffs, and Malvern Hill, in all of which he displayed a chivalrous courage. Afterward he became a signal officer and scout. "Nearly two years," he says, in speaking of this part of his service, "were passed in skirmishes, racing to escape the enemy's gunboats, signaling dispatches, serenading country beauties, poring over chance books, and foraging for provender." In 1864 he became a blockade runner, and in his first run out from near Fort Fisher, he was captured and taken to Point Lookout prison.

It is remarkable that, amid the distractions and hardships of active service, his love of music and letters triumphantly asserted itself. His flute was his constant companion. He utilized the brief intervals of repose that came to him in camp to set some of Tennyson's songs to music and to prosecute new lines of literary study. He took up the study of German, in which he became quite proficient, and by the light of the camp fire at night translated from Heine, Schiller, and Goethe. At the same time his sympathy with the varied aspects of Nature was deepened. Trees and flowers and ferns revealed to him their mystic beauty; and like Wordsworth, he found it easy, "in the lily, the sunset, the mountain, and rosy hues of all life, to trace God."

It was during his campaigns in Virginia that he began the composition of his only novel, *Tiger Lilies*, which was not completed, however, till 1867. It is now out of print. Though immature and somewhat chaotic, it clearly reveals the imaginative temperament of the author. War is imaged to his mind as "a strange, enormous, terrible flower," which he wishes might be eradicated forever and ever. As might be expected, music finds an honored place in its pages. He regards music as essential to the home. "Given the raw materials," he says, " to wit, wife, children, a friend or two, and a house, — two other things are necessary. These are a good fire and good music. And inasmuch as we can do without the fire for half the year, I may say that music is the one essen-

tial. After the evening spent around the piano,
or the flute, or the violin, how warm and how
chastened is the kiss with which the family all
say good night !   Ah, the music has taken all the
day cares and thrown them into its terrible alembic
and boiled them and rocked them and cooled them,
till they are crystallized into one care, which is a
most sweet and rare desirable sorrow — the yearning for God."

After the war came a rude struggle for existence — a struggle in which tuberculosis, contracted
during his camp life, gradually sapped his strength.
Hemorrhages became not infrequent, and he was
driven from one locality to another in a vain
search for health.   But he never lost hope ; and
his sufferings served to bring out his indomitable,
heroic spirit, and to stimulate him to the highest
degree of intellectual activity.   Few men have accomplished more when so heavily handicapped by
disease and poverty.   The record of his struggle
is truly pathetic.   In a letter to Paul Hamilton
Hayne, written in 1880, he gives us a glimpse
both of his physical suffering and his mental
agony.   " I could never tell you," he says, " the
extremity of illness, of poverty, and of unceasing
toil, in which I have spent the last three years,
and you would need only once to see the weariness
with which I crawl to bed after a long day's work,
and after a long night's work at the heels of it —
and Sundays just as well as other days — in order
to find in your heart a full warrant for my silence.
It seems incredible that I have printed such an

unchristian quantity of matter — all, too, tolerably
successful — and secured so little money ; and the
wife and the four boys, who are so lovely that I
would not think a palace good enough for them if
I had it, make one's earnings seem all the less."
During all these years of toil he longed to be
delivered from the hard struggle for bread that
he might give himself more fully to music and
poetry.

In 1867, while in charge of a prosperous school
at Prattville, Alabama, he married Miss Mary Day,
of Macon, Georgia. It proved a union in which
Lanier found perpetual inspiration and comfort.
His new-found strength and happiness are reflected
in more than one of his poems. In *Acknowledgment* we read : —

> " By the more height of thy sweet stature grown,
>   Twice-eyed with thy gray vision set in mine,
> I ken far lands to wifeless men unknown,
>   I compass stars for one-sexed eyes too fine."

And in *My Springs*, he says again, with great
beauty : —

> " Dear eyes, dear eyes and rare complete —
>   Being heavenly-sweet and earthly-sweet —
> I marvel that God made you mine,
>   For when He frowns, 'tis then ye shine ! "

In 1873, after giving up the study of law in his
father's office, he went to Baltimore, where he was
engaged as first flute for the Peabody Symphony
concerts. This engagement was a bold under-

taking, which cannot be better presented than in his own words. In a letter to Hayne he says: "Aside from the complete *bouleversement* of proceeding from the courthouse to the footlights, I was a raw player and a provincial withal, without practice, and guiltless of instruction — for I had never had a teacher. To go under these circumstances among old professional players, and assume a leading part in a large orchestra which was organized expressly to play the most difficult works of the great masters, was (now that it's all over) a piece of temerity that I don't remember ever to have equaled before. But I trusted in love, pure and simple, and was not disappointed; for, as if by miracle, difficulties and discouragements melted away before the fire of a passion for music which grows ever stronger within my heart; and I came out with results more gratifying than it is becoming in me to specify." His playing possessed an exquisite charm. "In his hands the flute," to quote from the tribute paid him by his director, "no longer remained a mere material instrument, but was transformed into a voice that set heavenly harmonies into vibration. Its tones developed colors, warmth, and a low sweetness of unspeakable poetry; they were not only true and pure, but poetic, allegoric as it were, suggestive of the depths and heights of being and of the delights which the earthly ear never hears and the earthly eye never sees."

Henceforth Baltimore was to be Lanier's home.

In addition to music, he gave himself seriously to literature. Before this period he had written a number of poems, limited in range and somewhat labored in manner. The current of his life still set to music, and his poetic efforts seem to have been less a matter of inspiration than of deliberate choice. In literary form the influence of Poe is discernible; but in subject-matter the sounds and colors of Nature, as in the poetry of his later years, occupy a prominent place. Of the poems of this early period the songs for *The Jacquerie* are the best. Here is a stanza of *Betrayal*: —

> " The sun has kissed the violet sea,
>   And burned the violet to a rose.
> O sea ! wouldst thou not better be
>   More violet still ? Who knows ? Who knows ?
>   Well hides the violet in the wood :
>   The dead leaf wrinkles her a hood,
>   And winter's ill is violet's good ;
>   But the bold glory of the rose,
>   It quickly comes and quickly goes —
>   Red petals whirling in white snows,
>   Ah me ! "

After taking up his residence in Baltimore, Lanier entered upon a comprehensive course of reading and study, particularly in early English literature. He studied Anglo-Saxon, and familiarized himself with Langland and Chaucer. He understood that any great poetic achievement must be based on extensive knowledge. A sweet warbler may depend on momentary inspiration;

but the great singer, who is to instruct and move
his age, must possess the insight and breadth of
vision that come alone from a profound acquaintance with Nature and human history. With keen
critical discernment Lanier said that "the trouble
with Poe was, he did not *know* enough. He
needed to know a good many more things in order
to be a great poet." It was to prepare himself for
the highest flights possible to him that he entered,
with inextinguishable ardor, upon a wide course of
reading.

In 1874 he was commissioned by a railroad company to write up the scenery, climate, and history
of Florida. While spending a month or two
with his family in Georgia, he wrote *Corn*, which
deservedly ranks as one of his noblest poems.
The delicate forms and colors of Nature touched
him to an ecstasy of delight; and at the same
time they bodied forth to his imagination deep
spiritual truths. As we read this poem, we feel
that the poet has reached a height of which little
promise is given in his earlier poems. Here are
the opening lines : —

" To-day the woods are trembling through and through
With shimmering forms, and flash before my view,
Then melt in green as dawn-stars melt in blue.
The leaves that wave against my cheek caress
Like women's hands ; the embracing boughs express
A subtlety of mighty tenderness ;
The copse-depths into little noises start,
That sound anon like beatings of a heart,
Anon like talk 'twixt lips not far apart.

The beach dreams balm, as a dreamer hums a song;
Through that vague wafture, expirations strong
Throb from young hickories breathing deep and long
With stress and urgence bold of prisoned spring
    And ecstasy burgeoning."

This poem is remarkable, too, for its presentation of Lanier's conception of the poetic office. The poet should be a prophet and leader, arousing mankind to all noble truth and action: —

"Look, out of line one tall corn-captain stands
  Advanced beyond the foremost of his bands,
    And waves his blades upon the very edge
    And hottest thicket of the battling hedge.
  Thou lustrous stalk, that ne'er mayst walk nor talk,
    Still shalt thou type the poet-soul sublime
    That leads the vanward of his timid time,
    And sings up cowards with commanding rhyme —
Soul calm, like thee, yet fain, like thee, to grow
By double increment, above, below;
    Soul homely, as thou art, yet rich in grace like thee,
    Teaching the yeomen selfless chivalry
    That moves in gentle curves of courtesy;
Soul filled like thy long veins with sweetness tense,
      By every godlike sense
Transmuted from the four wild elements."

For a time Lanier had difficulty in finding a publisher. He made a visit to New York, but met only with rebuffs. But upheld, like Wordsworth, by a strong consciousness of the excellence of his work, he did not lose his cheerful hope and courage.
The more I am thrown against these people here,

and the more reverses I suffer at their hands, the more confident I am of beating them finally. I do not mean by 'beating' that I am in opposition to them, or that I hate them or feel aggrieved with them; no, they know no better and they act up to their light with wonderful energy and consistency. I only mean that I am sure of being able, some day, to teach them better things and nobler modes of thought and conduct." *Corn* finally appeared in *Lippincott's Magazine* for February, 1875.

From this time poetry became a larger part of Lanier's life. His poetic genius had attained to fullness of power. He gave freer rein to imagination and thought and expression. Speaking of *Special Pleading*, which was written in 1875, he says : " In this little song, I have begun to dare to give myself some freedom in my own peculiar style, and have allowed myself to treat words, similes, and meters with such freedom as I desired. The result convinces me that I can do so now safely." In the next two or three years he produced such notable poems as *The Song of the Chattahoochee*, *The Symphony*, *The Revenge of Hamish*, *Clover*, *The Bee*, and *The Waving of the Corn*. They slowly gained recognition, and brought him the fellowship and encouragement of not a few literary people of distinction, among whom Bayard Taylor and Edmund Clarence Stedman deserve especial mention.

Perhaps none of Lanier's poems has been more popular than *The Song of the Chattahoochee*. It does not reach the poetic heights of a few of his other poems, but it is perfectly clear, and has a pleasant lilting movement. Moreover, it teaches the important truth that we are to be dumb to the siren voices of ease and pleasure when the stern voice of duty calls. The concluding stanza is as follows : —

> " But oh, not the hills of Habersham,
>　　And oh, not the valleys of Hall,
> Shall hinder the rain from attaining the plain,
>　　For downward the voices of duty call —
> Downward to toil and be mixed with the main.
> The dry fields burn and the mills are to turn,
> And a thousand meadows mortally yearn,
>　　And the final main from beyond the plain
>　　　Calls o'er the hills of Habersham,
>　　　And calls through the valleys of Hall."

In 1876, upon the recommendation of Bayard Taylor, Lanier was invited to write the centennial *Cantata*. As a poem, not much can be said in its favor. Its thought and form fall far below its ambitious conception, in which Columbia presents a meditation on the completed century of our country's history. On its publication it was subject to a good deal of unfavorable criticism ; but through it all, though it must have been a bitter disappointment, the poet never lost his faith in his genius and destiny. "The artist shall put forth, humbly and lovingly," he wrote to his father, "and without bitterness against opposition, the very best and highest that is within him, utterly regardless of contemporary criticism. What possible claim

can contemporary criticism set up to respect —
that criticism which crucified Jesus Christ, stoned
Stephen, hooted Paul for a madman, tried Luther
for a criminal, tortured Galileo, bound Columbus
in chains, and drove Dante into a hell of exile ?"

The need of a regular income became more and
more a necessity. "My head and my heart," he
wrote, "are both so full of poems, which the dreadful struggle for bread does not give me time to put
on paper, that I am often driven to headache and
heartache purely for want of an hour or two to
hold a pen." He sought various positions — a
clerkship in Washington, an assistant's place in
the Peabody Library, a consulship in the south of
France — all in vain. He lectured to parlor classes
in literature — an enterprise from which he seems
to have derived more fame than money. Finally,
in 1879, he was appointed to a lectureship in
English literature in Johns Hopkins University,
from which dates the final period of his literary
activity and of his life.

The first fruits of this appointment were a series
of lectures on metrical forms, which appeared, in
1880, in a volume entitled *The Science of English
Verse*. It is an original and suggestive work, in
which, however, the author's predilections for music
carry him too far. He has done well to emphasize
the time element in English versification ; but his
attempt to reduce all forms of verse to a musical
notation can hardly be regarded as successful.
His work, though comprehensive in scope, was not
intended to impose a new set of laws upon the

poet. " For the artist in verse," he says in his brief
concluding chapter, "there is no law: the perception and love of beauty constitute the whole
outfit; and what is herein set forth is to be taken
merely as enlarging that perception and exalting
that love. In all cases, the appeal is to the ear;
but the ear should, for that purpose, be educated
up to the highest possible plane of culture."

A second series of lectures, composed and
delivered when the anguish of mortal illness was
upon him, was subsequently published under the
title, *The English Novel.* Its aim was to trace
the development of personality in literature. It
contains much suggestive and sound criticism.
He did not share the fear entertained by some of
his contemporaries, that science would gradually
abolish poetry. Many of the finest poems in our
language, as he pointed out, have been written
while the wonderful discoveries of recent science
were being made. "Now," he continues, "if we
examine the course and progress of this poetry,
born thus within the very grasp and maw of this
terrible science, it seems to me that we find — as
to the *substance* of poetry — a steadily increasing
confidence and joy in the mission of the poet, in
the sacredness of faith and love and duty and
friendship and marriage, and the sovereign fact of
man's personality, while as to the *form* of the
poetry, we find that just as science has pruned our
faith (to make it more faithful), so it has pruned
our poetic form and technic, cutting away much
unproductive wood and effloresence, and creating

finer reserves and richer yields." Among novelists he assigns the highest place to George Eliot, who " shows man what he may be in terms of what he is."

There are two poems of this closing period that exhibit Lanier's characteristic manner at its best. They are the high-water mark of his poetic achievement. They exemplify his musical theories of meter. They show the trend forced upon him by his innate love of music; and though he might have written much more, if his life had been prolonged, it is doubtful whether he would have produced anything finer. Any further effort at musical effects would probably have resulted in a kind of ecstatic rhapsody. The first of the poems in question is the *Marshes of Glynn*, descriptive of the sea marshes near the city of Brunswick, Georgia.

" Ye marshes, how candid and simple and nothing-
     withholding and free —
   Ye publish yourselves to the sky and offer yourselves
     to the sea !
   Tolerant plains, that suffer the sea and the rains and
     the sun,
   Ye spread and span like the catholic man who hath
     mightily won
   God out of knowledge, and good out of infinite pain,
   And sight out of blindness, and purity out of a stain."

The other poem of his closing period, *Sunrise*, his greatest production, was written during the high fever of his last illness. In the poet's collected works, it is placed first in the series called *Hymns of the Marshes*. At times it almost reaches the point of ecstasy. His love of Nature finds supreme utterance.

" In my sleep I was fain of their fellowship, fain
  Of the live-oak, the marsh, and the main.
The little green leaves would not let me alone in my
    sleep ;
Up-breathed from the marshes, a message of range and
    of sweep,
Interwoven with waftures of wild sea-liberties, drifting,
Came through the lapped leaves sifting, sifting,
  Came to the gates of sleep.
Then my thoughts, in the dark of the dungeon-keep
Of the Castle of Captives hid in the City of Sleep,
Upstarted, by twos and by threes assembling :
  The gates of sleep fell a-trembling
Like as the lips of a lady that forth falter *yes*,
     Shaken with happiness :
  The gates of sleep stood wide.

  *   *   *   *   *   *   *

" Oh, what if a sound should be made !
  Oh, what if a bound should be laid
To this bow-and-string tension of beauty and silence
    a-spring, —
To the bend of beauty the bow, or the hold of silence
    the string !
I fear me, I fear me yon dome of diaphanous gleam
Will break as a bubble o'erblown in a dream, —
Yon dome of too-tenuous tissues of space and of night,
Overweighted with stars, overfreighted with light,
Oversated with beauty and silence, will seem
  But a bubble that broke in a dream,
If a bound of degree to this grace be laid,
    Or a sound or a motion made."

Throughout his artistic life Lanier was true to the loftiest ideals. He did not separate artistic from moral beauty. To his sensitive spirit, the beauty of holiness and the holiness of beauty seemed interchangeable terms. He did not make the shallow cry of "art for art's sake" a pretext or excuse for moral taint. On the contrary, he maintained that all art should be the embodiment of truth, goodness, love. "Can not one say with authority," he inquires in one of his university lectures, "to the young artist, whether working in stone, in color, in tones, or in character-forms of the novel: so far from dreading that your moral purpose will interfere with your beautiful creation, go forward in the clear conviction that, unless you are suffused — soul and body, one might say — with that moral purpose which finds its largest expression in love — that is, the love of all things in their proper relation — unless you are suffused with this love, do not dare to meddle with beauty; unless you are suffused with beauty, do not dare to meddle with truth; unless you are suffused with truth, do not dare to meddle with goodness. In a word, unless you are suffused with truth, wisdom, goodness, and love, abandon the hope that the ages will accept you as an artist."

Through these years of high aspiration and manly endeavor, the poet and musician was waging a losing fight with consumption. He was finally driven to tent life in a high, pure atmosphere as his only hope. He first went to Asheville, North Carolina, and a little later to Lynn.

But his efforts to regain his health proved in vain; and on the 7th of September, 1881, the tragic struggle was brought to a close.

The time has hardly come to give a final judgment as to Lanier's place in American letters. He certainly deserves a place by the side of the very best poets of the South, and perhaps, as many believe, by the side of the greatest masters of American song. His genius had elements of originality equaled only by Poe. He had the high moral purpose of the artist-prophets; but his efforts after musical effects, as well as his untimely death, prevented the full fruitage of his admirable genius. Many of the poems that he has left us are lacking in spontaneity and artistic finish. Alliterative effects are sometimes obtrusive. His poetic theories, as presented in *The Science of English Verse*, often outstripped his execution. But, after all these abatements are made, it remains true that in a few pieces he has reached a trembling height of poetic and musical rapture that is unsurpassed in the whole range of American poetry.

FATHER RYAN.

CHAPTER VI

THE poems of Abram J. Ryan, better known as Father Ryan, are unambitious. The poet modestly wished to call them only verses; and, as he tells us, they "were written at random, — off and on, here, there, anywhere, — just as the mood came, with little of study and less of art, and always in a hurry." His poems do not exhibit a painstaking, polished art. They are largely emotional outpourings of a heart that readily found expression in fluent, melodious lays. The poet-priest understood their character too well to assign them a very high place in the realm of song; yet the wish he expressed, that they might echo from heart to heart, has been fulfilled in no small degree. In *Sentinel Songs* he says : —

> " I sing with a voice too low
>   To be heard beyond to-day,
> In minor keys of my people's woe,
>   But my songs pass away.

> " To-morrow hears them not —
>   To-morrow belongs to fame —
> My songs, like the birds', will be forgot,
>   And forgotten shall be my name.

" And yet who knows ?   Betimes
   The grandest songs depart,
While the gentle, humble, and low-toned rhymes
   Will echo from heart to heart."

But few facts are recorded of Father Ryan's life.   The memoir and the critique prefixed to the latest edition of his poems but poorly fulfill their design.   Besides the absence of detail, there is an evident lack of taste and breadth of view.   The poet's ecclesiastical relation is unduly magnified ; and the invidious comparisons made and the immoderate laudation expressed are far from agreeable.   But we are not left wholly at a loss.   With the few recorded facts of his life as guide, the poems of Father Ryan become an interesting and instructive autobiography.   He was a spontaneous singer whose inspiration came, not from distant fields of legend, history, science, but from his own experience ; and it is not difficult to read there a romance, or rather a tragedy, which imparts a deep pathos to his life.   His *interior* life, as reflected in his poems, is all of good report, in no point clashing with the moral excellence befitting the priestly office.

Abram J. Ryan was born in Norfolk, Virginia, August 15, 1839, whither his parents, natives of Ireland, had immigrated not long before.   He possessed the quick sensibilities characteristic of the Celtic race ; and his love for Ireland is reflected in a stout martial lyric entitled *Erin's Flag :* —

" Lift it up ! lift it up ! the old Banner of Green !
   The blood of its sons has but brightened its sheen ;

What though the tyrant has trampled it down,
Are its folds not emblazoned with deeds of renown?"

When he was seven or eight years old, his
parents removed to St. Louis. He is said to have
shown great aptitude in acquiring knowledge;
and his superior intellectual gifts, associated with
an unusual reverence for sacred things, early
indicated the priesthood as his future vocation.
In the autobiographic poem, *Their Story Runneth
Thus*, we have a picture of his youthful character.
With a warm heart, he had more than the change-
fulness of the Celtic temperament. In his boyhood, as throughout his maturity, he was strangely
restless. As he says himself : —

"The boy was full of moods.
Upon his soul and face the dark and bright
Were strangely intermingled. Hours would pass
Rippling with his bright prattle — and then, hours
Would come and go, and never hear a word
Fall from his lips, and never see a smile
Upon his face. He was so like a cloud
With ever-changeful hues."

When his preliminary training was ended, he entered the Roman Catholic seminary at Niagara, New
York. He was moved to the priesthood by a spirit
of deep consecration. The writer of his memoir
dwells on the regret with which he severed the ties
binding him to home. No doubt he loved and
honored his parents. But there was a still stronger
attachment, which, broken by his call to the priest-

hood, filled all his subsequent life with a conse-
crated sorrow.   It was his love for Ethel:—

" A fair, sweet girl, with great, brown, wond'ring eyes
  That seemed to listen just as if they held
  The gift of hearing with the power of sight."

The two lovers, forgetting the sacredness of true
human affection, had, with equal self-abnegation,
resolved to give themselves to the church, she as a
nun and he as a priest.   He has given a touching
picture of their last meeting :—

" One night in mid of May their faces met
  As pure as all the stars that gazed on them.
  They met to part from themselves and the world.
  Their hearts just touched to separate and bleed ;
  Their eyes were linked in look, while saddest tears
  Fell down, like rain, upon the cheeks of each :
  They were to meet no more.   Their hands were clasped
  To tear the clasp in twain ; and all the stars
  Looked proudly down on them, while shadows knelt,
  Or seemed to kneel, around them with the awe
  Evoked from any heart by sacrifice.
  And in the heart of that last parting hour
  Eternity was beating.   And he said :
  ' We part to go to Calvary and to God —
  This is our garden of Gethsemane ;
  And here we bow our heads and breathe His prayer
  Whose heart was bleeding, while the angels heard :
  Not my will, Father ! but Thine be done ! ' "

The Roman Catholic training and faith of Father
Ryan exerted a deep influence upon his poetry.

His ardent studies in the ancient languages and in
scholastic theology naturally withdrew his mind,
to a greater or less degree, from intimate communion with Nature. His poetry is principally
subjective. Nature enters it only in a subordinate
way; its forms and sounds and colors do not inspire in him the rapture found in Hayne and
Lanier. He not only treats of Scripture themes,
as in *St. Stephen*, *The Master's Voice*, and *A Christ-
mas Chant*, but he also finds subjects, not always
happily, in distinctive Roman Catholic dogma.
The Feast of the Assumption and *The Last of May*,
both in honor of the Virgin Mary, are sufficiently
poetic; but *The Feast of the Sacred Heart* is, in
parts, too prosaically literal in its treatment of
transubstantiation for any but the most believing
and devout of Roman Catholics.

On the breaking out of the Civil War, Father
Ryan entered the Confederate army as a chaplain,
though he sometimes served in the ranks. In
1863 he ministered to the inmates of a prison
in New Orleans during an epidemic of smallpox.
His martial songs, *The Sword of Robert Lee*, *The
Conquered Banner*, and *March of the Deathless
Dead*, have been dear to many Southern hearts.
He reverenced Lee as a peerless leader.

> " Forth from its scabbard ! How we prayed
>   That sword might victor be ;
> And when our triumph was delayed,
> And many a heart grew sore afraid,
> We still hoped on while gleamed the blade
>   Of noble Robert Lee.

" Forth from its scabbard all in vain
   Bright flashed the sword of Lee ;
'Tis shrouded now in its sheath again,
It sleeps the sleep of our noble slain,
Defeated, yet without a stain,
   Proudly and peacefully."

After four years of brave, bitter sacrifice beneath the Confederate flag, words like the following appealed strongly to the men and women who
loved *The Conquered Banner :* —

" Take that Banner down ! 'tis tattered ;
   Broken is its staff and shattered ;
   And the valiant hosts are scattered
      Over whom it floated high.
   Oh ! 'tis hard for us to fold it ;
   Hard to think there's none to hold it ;
   Hard that those who once unrolled it
      Now must furl it with a sigh.

" Furl that Banner !   True, 'tis gory,
   Yet 'tis wreathed around with glory.
   And 'twill live in song and story,
      Though its folds are in the dust :
   For its fame on brightest pages,
   Penned by poets and by sages,
   Shall go sounding down the ages —
      Furl its folds though now we must."

Father Ryan's devotion to the South was intense.   He long refused to accept the results of
the war.   The wrongs of the so-called Reconstruction period aroused his ardent indignation,

and found expression in his song. In *The Land We Love* he says, with evident reference to those days : —

> " Land where the victor's flag waves,
>   Where only the dead are the free !
> Each link of the chain that enslaves,
>   But binds us to them and to thee."

But during the epidemic of yellow fever in 1878, his heart was touched by the splendid generosity of the North; and, surrendering his sectional prejudice and animosity, he wrote *Reunited :* —

> " Purer than thy own white snow,
>   Nobler than thy mountains' height;
> Deeper than the ocean's flow,
>   Stronger than thy own proud might;
> O Northland ! to thy sister land,
> Was late thy mercy's generous deed and grand."

After the close of the Civil War, the restless temperament of the poet-priest asserted itself in numerous changes of residence. He was successively in Biloxi, Mississippi, Knoxville, Tennessee, and Augusta, Georgia. In the latter place he published for some three years the *Banner of the South*, a periodical that exerted no small influence on the thought of the state. In 1870 he became pastor of St. Mary's church in Mobile. Two years later he made a trip to Europe, of which we find interesting reminiscences in his poems. His visit to

Rome was the realization of a long-cherished desire. He was honored with an audience by Pope Pius IX, of whom he has given a graphic sketch : —

> " I saw his face to-day; he looks a chief
> Who fears nor human rage, nor human guile ;
> Upon his cheeks the twilight of a grief,
> But in that grief the starlight of a smile.
> Deep, gentle eyes, with drooping lids that tell
> They are the homes where tears of sorrow dwell;
> A low voice — strangely sweet — whose very tone
> Tells how these lips speak oft with God alone."

In Milan he was seriously ill. In his poem, *After Sickness*, we find an expression of his world-weariness and his longing for death: —

> " I nearly died, I almost touched the door
> That swings between forever and no more ;
> I think I heard the awful hinges grate,
> Hour after hour, while I did weary wait
> Death's coming ; but alas ! 'twas all in vain :
> The door half opened and then closed again."

As a priest Father Ryan was faithful to his duties. But whether ministering at the altar or making the rounds of his parish, his spirit frequently found utterance in song. In 1880 he published a volume of poems, to which only a few additions were subsequently made. The keynote of his poetry is struck in the opening piece, *Song of the Mystic*. He dwelt much in the " Valley of Silence."

" Do you ask me the place of the Valley,
     Ye hearts that are harrowed by care ?
It lieth afar between mountains,
     And God and His angels are there :
And one is the dark mount of Sorrow,
     And one the bright mountain of Prayer."

The prevailing tone of Father Ryan's poems is
one of sadness.   His harp rarely vibrated to cheerful strains.   What was the cause of this sadness ?
It may have been his keen sense of the tragic side
of human life ; it may have been the enduring
anguish that came from the crucified love of his
youth.   The poet himself refused to tell.   In
Lines — 1875, he says : —

" Go list to the voices of air, earth, and sea,
   And the voices that sound in the sky ;
   Their songs may be joyful to some, but to me
   There's a sigh in each chord and a sigh in each key,
   And thousands of sighs swell their grand melody.
   Ask them what ails them : they will not reply.
   They sigh — sigh forever — but never tell why.
   Why does your poetry sound like a sigh ?
   Their lips will not answer you ; neither shall I."

Yet, in spite of the prevailing tone of sorrow
and weariness, Father Ryan was no pessimist.   He
held that life has " more of sweet than gall " —

   " For every one : no matter who —
       Or what their lot — or high or low ;
   All hearts have clouds — but heaven's blue
       Wraps robes of bright around each woe ;
   And this is truest of the true :

" That joy is stronger here than grief,
    Fills more of life, far more of years,
And makes the reign of sorrow brief ;
    Gives more of smiles for less of tears.
Joy is life's tree — grief but its leaves."

Father Ryan conceived of the poet's office as
something seerlike or prophetic. With him, as
with all great poets, the message counted for
more than do rhythm and rhyme. Divorced from
truth, art seemed to him but a skeleton masque.
He preferred those melodies that rise on the wings
of thought, and come to human hearts with an
inspiration of faith and hope. He regarded genuine poets as the high priests of Nature. Their sensitive spirits, holding themselves aloof from common
things, habitually dwell upon the deeper mysteries
of life in something of a morbid loneliness. In
Poets he says : —

" They are all dreamers ; in the day and night
    Ever across their souls
The wondrous mystery of the dark or bright
    In mystic rhythm rolls.

" They live within themselves — they may not tell
    What lieth deepest there ;
Within their breast a heaven or a hell,
    Joy or tormenting care.

" They are the loneliest men that walk men's ways,
    No matter what they seem ;
The stars and sunlight of their nights and days
    Move over them in dream."

With Wordsworth, or rather with the great Apostle to the Gentiles, he held that Nature is but the vesture of God, beneath which may be discerned the divine glory and love. The visible seemed to him but an expression of the invisible.

> " For God is everywhere — and he doth find
> In every atom which His hand hath made
> A shrine to hide His presence, and reveal
> His name, love, power, to those who kneel
> In holy faith upon this bright below,
> And lift their eyes, thro' all this mystery,
> To catch the vision of the great beyond."

With this view of Nature, it was but natural that its sounds and forms — its birds and flowers — should inspire devotion. In *St. Mary's*, speaking of the songs and silences of Nature, he says:—

> " God comes close to me here —
> Back of ev'ry roseleaf there
> He is hiding — and the air
> Thrills with calls to holy prayer;
>   Earth grows far, and heaven near.
>
> " Every single flower is fraught
> With the very sweetest dreams,
> Under clouds or under gleams
> Changeful ever — yet meseems
>   On each leaf I read God's thought."

It can hardly be said that Father Ryan ever reaches far poetic heights. Neither in thought nor expression does he often rise above cultured commonplace. Fine artistic quality is supplanted by a sort of melodious fluency. Yet the form and tone of his poetry, nearly always in one pensive key, make a distinct impression, unlike that of any other American singer. "Religious feeling," it has been well said, "is dominant. The reader seems to be moving about in cathedral glooms, by dimly lighted altars, with sad procession of ghostly penitents and mourners fading into the darkness to the sad music of lamenting choirs. But the light which falls upon the gloom is the light of heaven, and amid tears and sighs, over farewells and crushed happiness, hope sings a vigorous though subdued strain." Having once caught his distinctive note of weary melancholy, we can recognize it among a chorus of a thousand singers. It is to his honor that he has achieved a distinctive place in American poetry.

His poetic craftsmanship is far from perfect. His artistic sense did not aspire to exquisite achievements. He delighted unduly in alliteration, assonance, and rhyming effects, all which he sometimes carried to excess. In the first stanza, for example, of *The Conquered Banner*, popular as it is, the rhyme effect seems somewhat overdone : —

> " Furl that Banner, for 'tis weary ;
>   Round its staff 'tis drooping dreary ;
>   Furl it, fold it, it is best ;
>   For there's not a man to *wave it*,
>   And there's not a sword to *save it*,
>   And there's not one left to *lave it*
>   In the blood which heroes *gave it* ;
>   And its foes now scorn and *brave it* ;
>   Furl it, hide it — let it rest."

Here and there, too, are unmistakable echoes of Poe, as in the following stanza from *At Last :* —

> " Into a temple vast and dim,
>   *Solemn and vast and dim*,
> Just when the last sweet Vesper Hymn
>   Was floating far away,
> With eyes that tabernacled tears —
>   *Her heart the home of tears* —
> And cheeks wan with the woes of years,
>   A woman went one day."

But in spite of these obvious defects, Father Ryan has been for years the most popular of Southern poets. His poems have passed through many editions, and there is still a large demand for them. They have something that outweighs their faults, and appeals strongly to the popular mind and heart. What is it? Perhaps it is impossible to answer this question fully. But in addition to the merits already pointed out, the work of Father Ryan is for the most part simple, spontaneous, and clear. It generally consists of brief lyrics devoted to the expression of a single mood or reflection. There is nothing in thought or style beyond the ready comprehension of the average reader. It does not require, as does the poetry of Browning, repeated and careful reading to render its meaning clear. It does not offend sensible people with its empty, overdone refinement. From beginning to end Father Ryan's poetry is a transparent casket, into which he has poured the richest treasures of a deeply sorrowing but noble Christian spirit.

Again, the pensive, moral tone of his poetry renders it attractive to many persons. He gives expression to the sad, reflective moods that are apt, especially in time of suffering or disappointment, to come to most of us. The moral sense of the American people is strong; and sometimes a comforting though commonplace truth from Nature is more pleasing than the most exquisite but superficial description of her beauties. How many have found solace in poems like *A Thought* : —

> " The waving rose, with every breath
>   Scents carelessly the summer air ;
> The wounded rose bleeds forth in death
>   A sweetness far more rich and rare.

> " It is a truth beyond our ken —
>   And yet a truth that all may read —
> It is with roses as with men,
>   The sweetest hearts are those that bleed.

> " The flower which Bethlehem saw bloom
>   Out of a heart all full of grace,
> Gave never forth its full perfume
>   Until the cross became its vase."

Then again, the poet-priest, as was becoming his character, deals with the mysteries of life. Much of our recent poetry is as trifling in theme as it is polished in workmanship. But Father Ryan habitually brings before us the profounder and sadder aspects of life. The truths of religion, the vicissitudes of human destiny, the tragedy of death — these are the themes in which he finds

his inspiration, and to which we all turn in our
most serious moments. And though the strain in
which he sings is attuned to tears, it is still illumined by a strength-giving faith and hope. When
we feel weighed down with a sense of pitiless law,
when fate seems to cross our holiest aspirations
with a ruthless hand, he bids us be of good cheer.

> " There is no fate — God's love
>   Is law beneath each law,
>   And law all laws above
>   Fore'er, without a flaw."

In 1883 Father Ryan, whose reputation had
been established by his volume of poems, undertook a lecturing tour through the North in the
interest of some charitable enterprise. At his
best he was an eloquent speaker. But during the
later years of his life impaired health interfered
with prolonged mental effort. His mission had
only a moderate degree of success. His sense of
weariness deepened, and his eyes turned longingly
to the life to come. In one of his later productions
he said : —

> " My feet are wearied, and my hands are tired,
>   My soul oppressed —
>   And I desire, what I have long desired —
>   Rest — only rest.
> *   *   *   *   *   *
> " And so I cry a weak and human cry,
>   So heart oppressed ;
>   And so I sigh a weak and human sigh
>   For rest — for rest."

At length, April 22, 1886, in a Franciscan monastery at Louisville, came the rest for which he had prayed. And in that higher life to which he passed, we may believe that he was welcomed by her to whom in youth he had given the tender name of Ullainee, and for whom, through all the years of a great sacrifice, his faithful heart had yearned with an inextinguishable human longing.

ILLUSTRATIVE SELECTIONS
WITH NOTES

SELECTION FROM FRANCIS SCOTT KEY

THE STAR-SPANGLED BANNER [1]

O SAY, can you see, by the dawn's early light,
    What so proudly we hailed at the twilight's last
        gleaming,
Whose broad stripes and bright stars, through the
        perilous fight,
    O'er the ramparts [2] we watched, were so gallantly
        streaming?
And the rockets' red glare, the bombs bursting in
        air,
Gave proof through the night that our flag was
        still there.
O say, does that star-spangled banner yet wave
O'er the land of the free and the home of the
        brave?

On the shore dimly seen thro' the mists of the
        deep,
    Where the foe's haughty host in dread silence
        reposes,[3]
What is that which the breeze, o'er the towering
        steep,
    As it fitfully blows, half conceals, half dis-
        closes?

1, 2, 3, etc., refer to the Notes, pp. 209–237.

Now it catches the gleam of the morning's first
      beam,
In full glory reflected now shines on the stream;
'Tis the star-spangled banner; O long may it wave
O'er the land of the free and the home of the
      brave!

And where is that band who so vauntingly swore
      That the havoc of war and the battle's confusion
A home and a country should leave us no more? [4]
      Their blood has washed out their foul footsteps'
      pollution.
No refuge could save the hireling and slave
From the terror of flight, or the gloom of the grave;
And the star-spangled banner in triumph doth
      wave
O'er the land of the free and the home of the
      brave.

O! thus be it ever, when freemen shall stand
      Between their loved homes and the war's deso-
      lation!
Blest with victory and peace, may the heav'n-
      rescued land
      Praise the power that hath made and preserv'd
      us a nation!
Then conquer we must, when our cause it is just,
And this be our motto — "*In God is our trust:*"
And the star-spangled banner in triumph shall
      wave
O'er the land of the free and the home of the
      brave.

SELECTIONS FROM RICHARD HENRY WILDE

STANZAS[1]

My life is like the summer rose,
   That opens to the morning sky,
But, ere the shades of evening close,
   Is scattered on the ground — to die![2]
Yet on the rose's humble bed
The sweetest dews of night are shed,
As if she wept the waste to see —
But none shall weep a tear for me!

My life is like the autumn leaf
   That trembles in the moon's pale ray:
Its hold is frail — its date is brief,
   Restless — and soon to pass away!
Yet, ere that leaf shall fall and fade,
The parent tree will mourn its shade,
The winds bewail the leafless tree —
But none shall breathe a sigh for me!

My life is like the prints, which feet
   Have left on Tampa's[3] desert strand;
Soon as the rising tide shall beat,
   All trace will vanish from the sand;

Yet, as if grieving to efface
All vestige of the human race,
On that lone shore loud moans the sea --
But none, alas! shall mourn for me!

A FAREWELL TO AMERICA [1]

FAREWELL, my more than fatherland! [2]
  Home of my heart and friends, adieu!
Lingering beside some foreign strand,
  How oft shall I remember you!
  How often, o'er the waters blue,
Send back a sigh to those I leave,
  The loving and beloved few,
Who grieve for me, — for whom I grieve!

We part! — no matter how we part,
  There are some thoughts we utter not,
Deep treasured in our inmost heart,
  Never revealed, and ne'er forgot!
  Why murmur at the common lot?
We part! — I speak not of the pain, —
  But when shall I each lovely spot,
And each loved face behold again?

It must be months, — it may be years, [3] —
  It may — but no! — I will not fill
Fond hearts with gloom, — fond eyes with tears,
  "Curious to shape uncertain ill."

Though humble, — few and far, — yet, still
Those hearts and eyes are ever dear;
   Theirs is the love no time can chill,
The truth no chance or change can sear!

All I have seen, and all I see,
   Only endears them more and more;
Friends cool, hopes fade, and hours flee,
   Affection lives when all is o'er!
   Farewell, my more than native shore!
I do not seek or hope to find,
   Roam where I will, what I deplore
To leave with them and thee behind!

SELECTION FROM GEORGE D. PRENTICE

THE CLOSING YEAR [1]

'Tis midnight's holy hour, and silence now
Is brooding like a gentle spirit o'er
The still and pulseless world. Hark! on the winds
The bell's deep tones are swelling, — 'tis the knell
Of the departed year.
                No funeral train
Is sweeping past; yet on the stream and wood,
With melancholy light, the moonbeams rest
Like a pale, spotless shroud; the air is stirred,
As by a mourner's sigh; and on yon cloud
That floats so still and placidly through heaven,
The spirits of the seasons seem to stand —
Young Spring, bright Summer, Autumn's solemn
    form,
And Winter with his aged locks — and breathe,
In mournful cadences that come abroad
Like the far wind-harp's wild and touching wail,
A melancholy dirge o'er the dead year,
Gone from the earth forever.
                      'Tis a time
For memory and for tears. Within the deep,
Still chambers of the heart a specter dim,
Whose tones are like the wizard voice of Time,

Heard from the tomb of ages, points its cold
And solemn finger to the beautiful
And holy visions that have passed away,
And left no shadow of their loveliness
On the dead waste of life.   That specter lifts
The coffin lid of Hope, and Joy, and Love,
And, bending mournfully above the pale,
Sweet forms that slumber there, scatters dead flowers
O'er what has passed to nothingness.

                              The year
Has gone, and with it many a glorious throng
Of happy dreams.   Its mark is on each brow,
Its shadow in each heart.   In its swift course
It waved its scepter o'er the beautiful, —
And they are not.   It laid its pallid hand
Upon the strong man, — and the haughty form
Is fallen, and the flashing eye is dim.
It trod the hall of revelry, where thronged
The bright and joyous, and the tearful wail
Of stricken ones is heard, where erst the song
And reckless shout resounded.   It passed o'er
The battle plain, where sword, and spear, and shield
Flashed in the light of midday — and the strength
Of serried hosts is shivered, and the grass,
Green from the soil of carnage, waves above
The crushed and mouldering skeleton.   It came
And faded like a wreath of mist at eve;
Yet, ere it melted in the viewless air,
It heralded its millions to their home
In the dim land of dreams.

                              Remorseless Time!
Fierce spirit of the glass and scythe! — what power

Can stay him in his silent course, or melt
His iron heart to pity ?   On, still on
He presses, and forever.   The proud bird,
The condor of the Andes, that can soar
Through heaven's unfathomable depths, or brave
The fury of the northern hurricane,
And bathe his plumage in the thunder's home,
Furls his broad wings at nightfall and sinks down
To rest upon his mountain crag — but Time
Knows not the weight of sleep or weariness,
And night's deep darkness has no chain to bind
His rushing pinions.   Revolutions sweep
O'er earth, like troubled visions o'er the breast
Of dreaming sorrow, — cities rise and sink
Like bubbles on the water, — fiery isles
Spring blazing from the ocean, and go back
To their mysterious caverns, — mountains rear
To heaven their bald and blackened cliffs, and bow
Their tall heads to the plain, — new empires rise,
Gathering the strength of hoary centuries,
And rush down like the Alpine avalanche,
Startling the nations, — and the very stars,
Yon bright and burning blazonry of God,
Glitter a while in their eternal depths,
And, like the Pleiad, loveliest of their train,
Shoot from their glorious spheres, and pass away [2]
To darkle in the trackless void, — yet Time,
Time, the tomb-builder, holds his fierce career,
Dark, stern, all-pitiless, and pauses not
Amid the mighty wrecks that strew his path
To sit and muse, like other conquerors,
Upon the fearful ruin he has wrought.

SELECTIONS FROM WILLIAM GILMORE SIMMS

THE LOST PLEIAD[1]

NOT in the sky,
Where it was seen
So long in eminence of light serene, —
Nor on the white tops of the glistering wave,
Nor down in mansions of the hidden deep,
Though beautiful in green
And crystal, its great caves of mystery, —
Shall the bright watcher have
Her place, and, as of old, high station keep!

Gone! gone!
Oh! nevermore, to cheer
The mariner, who holds his course alone
On the Atlantic, through the weary night,
When the stars turn to watchers, and do sleep,
Shall it again appear,
With the sweet-loving certainty of light,
Down shining on the shut eyes of the deep!

The upward-looking shepherd on the hills
Of Chaldea, night-returning with his flocks,
He wonders why her beauty doth not blaze,
Gladding his gaze, —
And, from his dreary watch along the rocks,
Guiding him homeward o'er the perilous ways!

How stands he waiting still, in a sad maze,
Much wondering, while the drowsy silence fills
The sorrowful vault!—how lingers, in the hope
    that night
May yet renew the expected and sweet light,
So natural to his sight![2]

And lone,
Where, at the first, in smiling love she shone,
Brood the once happy circle of bright stars :
How should they dream, until her fate was known,
That they were ever confiscate to death?[3]
That dark oblivion the pure beauty mars,
And, like the earth, its common bloom and breath,
That they should fall from high ;
Their lights grow blasted by a touch, and die,
All their concerted springs of harmony
Snapt rudely, and the generous music gone![4]

Ah! still the strain
Of wailing sweetness fills the saddening sky ;
The sister stars, lamenting in their pain
That one of the selected ones must die, —
Must vanish, when most lovely, from the rest!
Alas! 'tis ever thus the destiny.
Even Rapture's song hath evermore a tone
Of wailing, as for bliss too quickly gone.
The hope most precious is the soonest lost,
The flower most sweet is first to feel the frost.
Are not all short-lived things the loveliest?
And, like the pale star, shooting down the sky,
Look they not ever brightest, as they fly
From the lone sphere they blest!

THE SWAMP FOX [1]

WE follow where the Swamp Fox guides,
    His friends and merry men are we;
And when the troop of Tarleton [2] rides,
    We burrow in the cypress tree.
The turfy hammock is our bed,
    Our home is in the red deer's den,
Our roof, the tree-top overhead,
    For we are wild and hunted men.

We fly by day and shun its light,
    But, prompt to strike the sudden blow,
We mount and start with early night,
    And through the forest track our foe. [3]
And soon he hears our chargers leap,
    The flashing saber blinds his eyes,
And ere he drives away his sleep,
    And rushes from his camp, he dies.

Free bridle bit, good gallant steed,
    That will not ask a kind caress
To swim the Santee [4] at our need,
    When on his heels the foemen press, —
The true heart and the ready hand,
    The spirit stubborn to be free,
The twisted bore, the smiting brand, —
    And we are Marion's men, you see.

Now light the fire and cook the meal,
    The last, perhaps, that we shall taste;
I hear the Swamp Fox round us steal,
    And that's a sign we move in haste.

He whistles to the scouts, and hark !
　You hear his order calm and low.
Come, wave your torch across the dark,
　And let us see the boys that go.

We may not see their forms again,
　God help 'em, should they find the strife !
For they are strong and fearless men,
　And make no coward terms for life ;
They'll fight as long as Marion bids,
　And when he speaks the word to shy,
Then, not till then, they turn their steeds,
　Through thickening shade and swamp to fly.

Now stir the fire and lie at ease, —
　The scouts are gone, and on the brush
I see the Colonel[5] bend his knees,
　To take his slumbers too.   But hush !
He's praying, comrades ; 'tis not strange ;
　The man that's fighting day by day
May well, when night comes, take a change,
　And down upon his knees to pray.

Break up that hoecake, boys, and hand
　The sly and silent jug that's there ;
I love not it should idly stand
　When Marion's men have need of cheer.
'Tis seldom that our luck affords
　A stuff like this we just have quaffed,
And dry potatoes on our boards
　May always call for such a draught.

Now pile the brush and roll the log ;
   Hard pillow, but a soldier's head
That's half the time in brake and bog
   Must never think of softer bed.
The owl is hooting to the night,
   The cooter [6] crawling o'er the bank,
And in that pond the flashing light
   Tells where the alligator sank.

What ! 'tis the signal ! start so soon,
   And through the Santee swamp so deep,
Without the aid of friendly moon,
   And we, Heaven help us ! half asleep !
But courage, comrades !   Marion leads,
   The Swamp Fox takes us out to-night;
So clear your swords and spur your steeds,
   There's goodly chance, I think, of fight.

We follow where the Swamp Fox guides,
   We leave the swamp and cypress tree,
Our spurs are in our coursers' sides,
   And ready for the strife are we.
The Tory camp is now in sight,
   And there he cowers within his den ;
He hears our shouts, he dreads the fight,
   He fears, and flies from Marion's men.

SELECTIONS FROM EDWARD COATE PINKNEY

A HEALTH [1]

I FILL this cup to one made up
  Of loveliness alone,
A woman, of her gentle sex
  The seeming paragon;
To whom the better elements
  And kindly stars have given
A form so fair, that, like the air,
  'Tis less of earth than heaven.

Her every tone is music's own,
  Like those of morning birds,
And something more than melody
  Dwells ever in her words;
The coinage of her heart are they,
  And from her lips each flows
As one may see the burdened bee
  Forth issue from the rose.

Affections are as thoughts to her,[2]
  The measures of her hours;
Her feelings have the fragrancy,
  The freshness of young flowers;

And lovely passions, changing oft,
    So fill her, she appears
The image of themselves by turns, —
    The idol of past years !

Of her bright face one glance will trace
    A picture on the brain,
And of her voice in echoing hearts
    A sound must long remain;
But memory, such as mine of her,
    So very much endears,
When death is nigh my latest sigh
    Will not be life's, but hers.

I fill this cup to one made up
    Of loveliness alone,
A woman, of her gentle sex
    The seeming paragon —
Her health ! and would on earth there stood
    Some more of such a frame,
That life might be all poetry,
    And weariness a name.[3]

SONG

WE break the glass, whose sacred wine
    To some beloved health we drain,
Lest future pledges, less divine,
    Should e'er the hallowed toy profane;
And thus I broke a heart that poured
    Its tide of feelings out for thee,
In draught, by after-times deplored,
    Yet dear to memory.

But still the old, impassioned ways
　　And habits of my mind remain,
And still unhappy light displays
　　Thine image chambered in my brain;
And still it looks as when the hours
　　Went by like flights of singing birds,[1]
Or that soft chain of spoken flowers
　　And airy gems, — thy words.

VOTIVE SONG

I BURN no incense, hang no wreath,
　　On this thine early tomb:
Such can not cheer the place of death,
　　But only mock its gloom.
Here odorous smoke and breathing flower
　　No grateful influence shed;
They lose their perfume and their power,
　　When offered to the dead.

And if, as is the Afghaun's creed,
　　The spirit may return,
A disembodied sense to feed
　　On fragrance, near its urn, —
It is enough that she, whom thou
　　Didst love in living years,
Sits desolate beside it now,
　　And fall these heavy tears.

SELECTION FROM PHILIP PENDLETON COOKE

FLORENCE VANE [1]

I LOVED thee long and dearly,
    Florence Vane;
My life's bright dream, and early,
    Hath come again;
I renew, in my fond vision,
    My heart's dear pain;
My hope, and thy derision,
    Florence Vane.

The ruin lone and hoary,
    The ruin old,
Where thou didst hark my story,
    At even told, —
That spot — the hues Elysian
    Of sky and plain —
I treasure in my vision,
    Florence Vane.

Thou wast lovelier than the roses
    In their prime;
Thy voice excelled the closes
    Of sweetest rhyme;

Thy heart was as a river
   Without a main.[2]
Would I had loved thee never,
   Florence Vane.

But fairest, coldest wonder!
   Thy glorious clay
Lieth the green sod under —
   Alas the day!
And it boots not to remember
   Thy disdain —
To quicken love's pale ember,
   Florence Vane.

The lilies of the valley
   By young graves weep,
The pansies love to dally
   Where maidens sleep;
May their bloom, in beauty vying,
   Never wane,
Where thine earthly part is lying,
   Florence Vane!

SELECTION FROM THEODORE O'HARA

THE BIVOUAC OF THE DEAD [1]

THE muffled drum's sad roll has beat
    The soldier's last tattoo:
No more on Life's parade shall meet
    That brave and fallen few.
On Fame's eternal camping-ground
    Their silent tents are spread,
And Glory guards, with solemn round,
    The bivouac of the dead.

No rumor of the foe's advance
    Now swells upon the wind;
No troubled thought at midnight haunts
    Of loved ones left behind;
No vision of the morrow's strife
    The warrior's dream alarms;
No braying horn nor screaming fife
    At dawn shall call to arms.

Their shivered swords are red with rust,
    Their plumèd heads are bowed;
Their haughty banner, trailed in dust,
    Is now their martial shroud.

And plenteous funeral tears have washed
  The red stains from each brow,
And the proud forms, by battle gashed,
  Are free from anguish now.

The neighing troop, the flashing blade,
  The bugle's stirring blast,
The charge, the dreadful cannonade,
  The din and shout, are past;
Nor war's wild note nor glory's peal
  Shall thrill with fierce delight
Those breasts that nevermore may feel
  The rapture of the fight.

Like the fierce northern hurricane
  That sweeps his great plateau,
Flushed with the triumph yet to gain,
  Came down the serried foe.[2]
Who heard the thunder of the fray
  Break o'er the field beneath,
Knew well the watchword of that day
  Was " Victory or Death."

Long had the doubtful conflict raged
  O'er all that stricken plain,
For never fiercer fight had waged
  The vengeful blood of Spain ; [3]
And still the storm of battle blew,
  Still swelled the gory tide ;
Not long, our stout old chieftain knew,
  Such odds his strength could bide.

'Twas in that hour his stern command
 Called to a martyr's grave
The flower of his beloved land,
 The nation's flag to save.
By rivers of their fathers' gore
 His first-born laurels grew,[4]
And well he deemed the sons would pour
 Their lives for glory too.

Full many a norther's breath has swept
 O'er Angostura's plain,[5]
And long the pitying sky has wept
 Above its moldered slain.
The raven's scream, or eagle's flight,
 Or shepherd's pensive lay,
Alone awakes each sullen height
 That frowned o'er that dread fray.

Sons of the Dark and Bloody Ground,
 Ye must not slumber there,
Where stranger steps and tongues resound
 Along the heedless air.
Your own proud land's heroic soil
 Shall be your fitter grave:
She claims from war his richest spoil —
 The ashes of her brave.

Thus 'neath their parent turf they rest,
 Far from the gory field,
Borne to a Spartan mother's breast
 On many a bloody shield;[6]

The sunshine of their native sky
  Smiles sadly on them here,
And kindred eyes and hearts watch by
  The heroes' sepulcher.

Rest on, embalmed and sainted dead!
  Dear as the blood ye gave;
No impious footstep here shall tread
  The herbage of your grave;
Nor shall your glory be forgot
  While Fame her record keeps,
Or Honor points the hallowed spot
  Where valor proudly sleeps.

Yon marble minstrel's voiceless stone
  In deathless song shall tell,
When many a vanished age hath flown,
  The story how ye fell;
Nor wreck, nor change, nor winter's blight,
  Nor Time's remorseless doom,
Shall dim one ray of glory's light
  That gilds your deathless tomb.

SELECTIONS FROM FRANCIS ORRERY TICKNOR

THE VIRGINIANS OF THE VALLEY [1]

THE knightliest of the knightly race
  That, since the days of old,
Have kept the lamp of chivalry
  Alight in hearts of gold;
The kindliest of the kindly band
  That, rarely hating ease,
Yet rode with Spotswood [2] round the land,
  With Raleigh round the seas;

Who climbed the blue Virginian hills
  Against embattled foes,
And planted there, in valleys fair,
  The lily and the rose;
Whose fragrance lives in many lands,
  Whose beauty stars the earth,
And lights the hearths of happy homes
  With loveliness and worth.

We thought they slept! — the sons who kept
  The names of noble sires,
And slumbered while the darkness crept
  Around their vigil fires;

But aye the "Golden Horseshoe" knights
  Their Old Dominion [3] keep,
Whose foes have found enchanted ground,
  But not a knight asleep.

LITTLE GIFFEN [1]

Out of the focal and foremost fire,
Out of the hospital walls as dire;
Smitten of grape-shot and gangrene,
(Eighteenth battle [2] and *he* sixteen!)
Specter! such as you seldom see,
Little Giffen, of Tennessee!

"Take him and welcome!" the surgeons said;
Little the doctor can help the dead!
So we took him; and brought him where
The balm was sweet in the summer air;
And we laid him down on a wholesome bed,—
Utter Lazarus, heel to head!

And we watched the war with abated breath,—
Skeleton Boy against skeleton Death.
Months of torture, how many such?
Weary weeks of the stick and crutch;
And still a glint of the steel-blue eye
Told of a spirit that wouldn't die,

And didn't. Nay, more! in death's despite
The crippled skeleton "learned to write."
"Dear Mother," at first, of course; and then
"Dear captain," inquiring about the men.
Captain's answer: "Of eighty-and-five,
Giffen and I are left alive."

Word of gloom from the war, one day;
Johnston pressed at the front, they say.
Little Giffen was up and away;
A tear — his first — as he bade good-by,
Dimmed the glint of his steel-blue eye.
"I'll write, if spared!" There was news of the
    fight;
But none of Giffen. — He did not write.[3]

I sometimes fancy that, were I king
Of the princely Knights of the Golden Ring,[4]
With the song of the minstrel in mine ear,
And the tender legend that trembles here,
I'd give the best on his bended knee,
The whitest soul of my chivalry,
For " Little Giffen," of Tennessee.

SELECTION FROM JOHN R. THOMPSON

MUSIC IN CAMP [1]

Two armies covered hill and plain,
  Where Rappahannock's waters [2]
Ran deeply crimsoned with the stain
  Of battle's recent slaughters.

The summer clouds lay pitched like tents
  In meads of heavenly azure ;
And each dread gun of the elements
  Slept in its hid embrasure.

The breeze so softly blew, it made
  No forest leaf to quiver,
And the smoke of the random cannonade
  Rolled slowly from the river.

And now, where circling hills looked down
  With cannon grimly planted,
O'er listless camp and silent town
  The golden sunset slanted.

When on the fervid air there came
  A strain — now rich, now tender ;
The music seemed itself aflame
  With day's departing splendor.

A Federal band, which, eve and morn,
   Played measures brave and nimble,
Had just struck up, with flute and horn
   And lively clash of cymbal.

Down flocked the soldiers to the banks,
   Till, margined by its pebbles,
One wooded shore was blue with " Yanks,"
   And one was gray with " Rebels."

Then all was still, and then the band,
   With movement light and tricksy,
Made stream and forest, hill and strand,
   Reverberate with " Dixie."

The conscious stream with burnished glow
   Went proudly o'er its pebbles,
But thrilled throughout its deepest flow
   With yelling of the Rebels.

Again a pause, and then again
   The trumpets pealed sonorous,
And "Yankee Doodle" was the strain
   To which the shore gave chorus.

The laughing ripple shoreward flew,
   To kiss the shining pebbles;
Loud shrieked the swarming Boys in Blue
   Defiance to the Rebels.

And yet once more the bugles sang
   Above the stormy riot;
No shout upon the evening rang —
   There reigned a holy quiet.

The sad, slow stream its noiseless flood
  Poured o'er the glistening pebbles;
All silent now the Yankees stood,
  And silent stood the Rebels.

No unresponsive soul had heard
  That plaintive note's appealing,
So deeply " Home, Sweet Home " had stirred
  The hidden founts of feeling.

Or Blue or Gray the soldier sees,
  As by the wand of fairy,
The cottage 'neath the live-oak trees,
  The cabin by the prairie.

Or cold or warm, his native skies
  Bend in their beauty o'er him;
Seen through the tear-mist in his eyes,
  His loved ones stand before him.

As fades the iris after rain
  In April's tearful weather,
The vision vanished, as the strain
  And daylight died together.

And memory, waked by music's art,
  Expressed in simplest numbers,
Subdued the sternest Yankee's heart,
  Made light the Rebel's slumbers.

And fair the form of music shines,
  That bright celestial creature,
Who still, 'mid war's embattled lines,
  Gave this one touch of Nature.

SELECTIONS FROM MRS. MARGARET J. PRESTON

Grateful acknowledgment is here made to Dr. George J. Preston of Baltimore, for permission to use the two following poems.

A NOVEMBER NOCTURNE [1]

THE autumn air sweeps faint and chill
Across the maple-crested hill;
    And on my ear
    Falls, tingling clear,
A strange, mysterious, woodland thrill.

From utmost twig, from scarlet crown
Untouched with yet a tint of brown,
    Reluctant, slow,
    As loath to go,
The loosened leaves come wavering down;

And not a hectic trembler there,
In its decadence, doomed to share
    The fate of all, —
    But in its fall
Flings something sob-like on the air.

No drift or dream of passing bell,
Dying afar in twilight dell,
    Hath any heard,
    Whose chimes have stirred
More yearning pathos of farewell.

A silent shiver as of pain,
Goes quivering through each sapless vein;
    And there are moans,
    Whose undertones
Are sad as midnight autumn rain.

Ah, if without its dirge-like sigh,
No lightest, clinging leaf can die, —
    Let him who saith
    Decay and death
Should bring no heart-break, tell me why.

Each graveyard gives the answer: there
I read *Resurgam*[2] everywhere,
    So easy said
    Above the dead —
So weak to anodyne despair.

CALLING THE ANGELS IN

WE mean to do it.   Some day, some day,
  We mean to slacken this feverish rush
That is wearing our very souls away,
  And grant to our hearts a hush
That is only enough to let them hear
The footsteps of angels drawing near.

We mean to do it.   Oh, never doubt,
  When the burden of daytime broil is o'er,
We'll sit and muse while the stars come out,
  As the patriarchs sat in the door[1]
Of their tents with a heavenward-gazing eye,
To watch for angels passing by.

We've seen them afar at high noontide,
　　When fiercely the world's hot flashings beat;
Yet never have bidden them turn aside,
　　To tarry in converse sweet;
Nor prayed them to hallow the cheer we spread,
To drink of our wine and break our bread.

We promise our hearts that when the stress
　　Of the life work reaches the longed-for close,
When the weight that we groan with hinders less,
　　We'll welcome such calm repose
As banishes care's disturbing din,
And then — we'll call the angels in.

The day that we dreamed of comes at length,
　　When tired of every mocking guest,
And broken in spirit and shorn of strength,
　　We drop at the door of rest,
And wait and watch as the day wanes on —
But the angels we meant to call are gone!

SELECTIONS FROM EDGAR ALLAN POE

TO HELEN [1]

HELEN, thy beauty is to me
   Like those Nicæan [2] barks of yore,
That gently, o'er a perfumed sea,
   The weary, wayworn wanderer bore
   To his own native shore.

On desperate seas long wont to roam,
   Thy hyacinth hair, thy classic face,
Thy Naiad airs, have brought me home
   To the glory that was Greece,
   And the grandeur that was Rome. [3]

Lo! in yon brilliant window-niche
   How statue-like I see thee stand,
The agate lamp within thy hand!
   Ah, Psyche, [4] from the regions which
   Are Holy Land!

ANNABEL LEE [1]

IT was many and many a year ago,
   In a kingdom by the sea, [2]
That a maiden there lived whom you may know
   By the name of Annabel Lee;
And this maiden she lived with no other thought
   Than to love and be loved by me.

I was a child and she was a child,
　　In this kingdom by the sea :
But we loved with a love that was more than
　　　love,
　　I and my Annabel Lee ;
With a love that the winged seraphs of heaven
　　Coveted her and me.[3]

And this was the reason that, long ago,
　　In this kingdom by the sea,
A wind blew out of a cloud, chilling
　　My beautiful Annabel Lee ;
So that her highborn kinsmen [4] came
　　And bore her away from me,
To shut her up in a sepulcher
　　In this kingdom by the sea.

The angels, not half so happy in heaven,
　　Went envying her and me ;
Yes ! — that was the reason (as all men know,
　　In this kingdom by the sea)
That the wind came out of the cloud by night,
　　Chilling and killing my Annabel Lee.

But our love it was stronger by far than the love
　　Of those who were older than we,
　　Of many far wiser than we ;
And neither the angels in heaven above,
　　Nor the demons down under the sea,
Can ever dissever my soul from the soul
　　Of the beautiful Annabel Lee :

For the moon never beams without bringing me
    dreams
  Of the beautiful Annabel Lee;
And the stars never rise, but I feel the bright
    eyes
  Of the beautiful Annabel Lee;
And so, all the night-tide, I lie down by the side[5]
Of my darling — my darling — my life and my
    bride,
  In her sepulcher there by the sea,
  In her tomb by the sounding sea.

THE HAUNTED PALACE[1]

In the greenest of our valleys
  By good angels tenanted,
Once a fair and stately palace —
  Radiant palace — reared its head.
In the monarch Thought's dominion,
  It stood there;
Never seraph spread a pinion
  Over fabric half so fair.

Banners yellow, glorious, golden,
  On its roof did float and flow
(This — all this — was in the olden
  Time long ago),
And every gentle air that dallied,
  In that sweet day,
Along the ramparts plumed and pallid,
  A wingèd odor went away.

Wanderers in that happy valley
   Through two luminous windows saw
Spirits moving musically,
   To a lute's well-tunèd law,
Round about a throne where, sitting,
   Porphyrogene,
In state his glory well befitting,
   The ruler of the realm was seen.

And all with pearl and ruby glowing
   Was the fair palace door,
Through which came flowing, flowing, flowing,
   And sparkling evermore,
A troop of Echoes, whose sweet duty
   Was but to sing,
In voices of surpassing beauty,
   The wit and wisdom of their king.

But evil things, in robes of sorrow,
   Assailed the monarch's high estate;
(Ah, let us mourn, for never morrow
   Shall dawn upon him desolate!)
And round about his home the glory
   That blushed and bloomed,
Is but a dim-remembered story
   Of the old time entombed.

And travelers now within that valley
   Through the red-litten windows see
Vast forms that move fantastically
   To a discordant melody;

While like a ghastly rapid river,
  Through the pale door
A hideous throng rush out forever,
  And laugh — but smile no more.

THE CONQUEROR WORM [1]

Lo! 'tis a gala night
  Within the lonesome latter years.
An angel throng, bewinged, bedight
  In veils, and drowned in tears,
Sit in a theater to see
  A play of hopes and fears,
While the orchestra breathes fitfully
  The music of the spheres.

Mimes, in the form of God on high,
  Mutter and mumble low,
And hither and thither fly;
  Mere puppets they, who come and go
At bidding of vast formless things
  That shift the scenery to and fro,
Flapping from out their condor wings
  Invisible woe.

That motley drama — oh, be sure
  It shall not be forgot!
With its Phantom chased for evermore
  By a crowd that seize it not,
Through a circle that ever returneth in
  To the self-same spot;
And much of Madness, and more of Sin,
  And Horror the soul of the plot.

But see amid the mimic rout
   A crawling shape intrude :
A blood-red thing that writhes from **out**
   The scenic solitude !
It writhes — it writhes ! — with mortal **pangs**
   The mimes become its food,
And seraphs sob at vermin fangs
   In human gore imbued.

Out — out are the lights — out all !
   And over each quivering form
The curtain, a funeral pall,
   Comes down with the rush of a **storm,**
While the angels, all pallid and wan,
   Uprising, unveiling, affirm
That the play is the tragedy " Man,"
   And its hero the Conqueror **Worm.**

THE RAVEN [1]

ONCE upon a midnight dreary, while I pondered,
   weak and weary,
Over many a quaint and curious volume of forgotten lore, —
While I nodded, nearly napping, suddenly there
   came a tapping,
As of some one gently rapping, rapping at my
   chamber door.
" 'Tis some visitor," I muttered, " tapping at my
   chamber door —
       Only this and nothing more."

Ah, distinctly I remember it was in the bleak
  December,
And each separate dying ember wrought its ghost
  upon the floor.
Eagerly I wished the morrow; — vainly I had
  sought to borrow
From my books surcease of sorrow — sorrow for
  the lost Lenore,
For the rare and radiant maiden whom the angels
  name Lenore:
  Nameless here for evermore.

And the silken sad uncertain rustling of each
  purple curtain
Thrilled me — filled me with fantastic terrors never
  felt before;
So that now, to still the beating of my heart, I
  stood repeating
"'Tis some visitor entreating entrance at my
  chamber door —
Some late visitor entreating entrance at my chamber door:
  This it is and nothing more."

Presently my soul grew stronger; hesitating then
  no longer,
"Sir," said I, " or Madam, truly your forgiveness
  I implore;
But the fact is I was napping, and so gently you
  came rapping,
And so faintly you came tapping, tapping at my
  chamber door,

That I scarce was sure I heard you " — here I
    opened wide the door; —
        Darkness there and nothing more.

Deep into the darkness peering, long I stood there
    wondering, fearing,
Doubting, dreaming dreams no mortal ever dared
    to dream before ;
But the silence was unbroken, and the stillness
    gave no token,
And the only word there spoken was the whis-
    pered word " Lenore ? "
This I whispered, and an echo murmured back the
    word " Lenore : "
        Merely this and nothing more.

Back into the chamber turning, all my soul within
    me burning,
Soon again I heard a tapping somewhat louder
    than before.
" Surely," said I, "surely that is something at my
    window lattice ;
Let me see, then, what thereat is, and this mys-
    tery explore —
Let my heart be still a moment and this mystery
    explore :
        'Tis the wind and nothing more."

Open here I flung the shutter, when, with many a
    flirt and flutter,
In there stepped a stately Raven of the saintly
    days of yore.

Not the least obeisance made he; not a minute
    stopped or stayed he;
But with mien of lord or lady, perched above my
    chamber door —
Perched upon a bust of Pallas just above my
    chamber door:
        Perched, and sat, and nothing more.

Then this ebony bird beguiling my sad fancy into
    smiling,
By the grave and stern decorum of the counte-
    nance it wore, —
" Though thy crest be shorn and shaven, thou," I
    said, " art sure no craven,
Ghastly grim and ancient Raven wandering from
    the Nightly shore:
Tell me what thy lordly name is on the Night's
    Plutonian shore!"
        Quoth the Raven, " Nevermore."

Much I marveled this ungainly fowl to hear dis-
    course so plainly,
Though its answer little meaning — little relevancy
    bore;
For we cannot help agreeing that no living human
    being
Ever yet was blessed with seeing bird above his
    chamber door —
Bird or beast upon the sculptured bust above his
    chamber door,
        With such name as " Nevermore."

But the Raven, sitting lonely on that placid bust,
    spoke only
That one word, as if his soul in that one word he
    did outpour.
Nothing farther then he uttered; not a feather
    then he fluttered,
Till I scarcely more than muttered, — "Other
    friends have flown before ;
On the morrow *he* will leave me, as my Hopes
    have flown before."
        Then the bird said, " Nevermore."

Startled at the stillness broken by reply so aptly
    spoken,
" Doubtless," said I, "what it utters is its only
    stock and store,
Caught from some unhappy master whom unmer-
    ciful Disaster
Followed fast and followed faster till his songs
    one burden bore :
Till the dirges of his Hope that melancholy burden
    bore
        Of ' Never — nevermore.' "

But the Raven still beguiling all my sad soul into
    smiling,
Straight I wheeled a cushioned seat in front of
    bird and bust and door ;
Then, upon the velvet sinking, I betook myself to
    linking
Fancy unto fancy, thinking what this ominous bird
    of yore,

What this grim, ungainly, ghastly, gaunt, and
    ominous bird of yore —
        Meant in croaking "Nevermore."

This I sat engaged in guessing, but no syllable
    expressing
To the fowl whose fiery eyes now burned into my
    bosom's core ;
This and more I sat divining, with my head at
    ease reclining
On the cushion's velvet lining that the lamplight
    gloated o'er,
But whose velvet violet lining with the lamplight
    gloating o'er
        She shall press, ah, nevermore !

Then, methought, the air grew denser, perfumed
    from an unseen censer
Swung by seraphim whose footfalls tinkled on the
    tufted floor.
"Wretch," I cried, " thy God hath lent thee — by
    these angels he hath sent thee
Respite — respite and nepenthe from thy memo-
    ries of Lenore !
Quaff, oh quaff this kind nepenthe and forget this
    lost Lenore ! "
        Quoth the Raven, " Nevermore."

"Prophet!" said I, "thing of evil! prophet still,
    if bird or devil !
Whether Tempter sent, or whether tempest tossed
    thee here ashore,

Desolate yet all undaunted, on this desert land
  enchanted —
On this home by Horror haunted — tell me truly, I
  implore :
Is there — *is* there balm in Gilead? — tell me —
  tell me, I implore ! "
    Quoth the Raven, " Nevermore."

" Prophet ! " said I, " thing of evil — prophet still,
  if bird or devil !
By that heaven that bends above us — by that God
  we both adore :
Tell this soul with sorrow laden if, within the distant Aidenn,
It shall clasp a sainted maiden whom the angels
  name Lenore :
Clasp a rare and radiant maiden whom the angels
  name Lenore ! "
    Quoth the Raven, " Nevermore."

" Be that word our sign of parting, bird or fiend ! "
  I shrieked, upstarting :
" Get thee back into the tempest and the Night's
  Plutonian shore !
Leave no black plume as a token of that lie thy
  soul hath spoken !
Leave my loneliness unbroken ! quit the bust above
  my door !
Take thy beak from out my heart, and take thy
  form from off my door ! "
    Quoth the Raven, " Nevermore."

And the Raven, never flitting, still is sitting, still
    is sitting
On the pallid bust of Pallas just above my chamber
    door ; [2]
And his eyes have all the seeming of a demon's
    that is dreaming,
And the lamplight o'er him streaming throws his
    shadow on the floor ; [3]
And my soul from out that shadow that lies float-
    ing on the floor
        Shall be lifted — nevermore !

SELECTIONS FROM PAUL HAMILTON HAYNE

For their generous permission to use *Aëthra*, *Under the Pines*, *Cloud Pictures*, and *Lyric of Action*, the grateful acknowledgments of the editor are due to The Lothrop Publishing Company, Boston, who hold the copyright.

THE WILL AND THE WING [1]

To have the will to soar, but not the wings,
　　Eyes fixed forever on a starry height,
Whence stately shapes of grand imaginings
　　Flash down the splendors of imperial light;

And yet to lack the charm [2] that makes them ours,
　　The obedient vassals of that conquering spell,
Whose omnipresent and ethereal powers
　　Encircle Heaven, nor fear to enter Hell;

This is the doom of Tantalus [3] — the thirst
　　For beauty's balmy fount to quench the fires
Of the wild passion that our souls have nurst
　　In hopeless promptings — unfulfilled desires.

Yet would I rather in the outward state
　　Of Song's immortal temple lay me down,
A beggar basking by that radiant gate, [4]
　　Than bend beneath the haughtiest empire's crown!

For sometimes, through the bars, my ravished eyes
 Have caught brief glimpses of a life divine,
And seen a far, mysterious rapture rise
 Beyond the veil[5] that guards the inmost shrine.

MY STUDY[1]

THIS is my world! within these narrow walls,
I own a princely service;[2] the hot care
And tumult of our frenzied life are here
But as a ghost and echo; what befalls
In the far mart to me is less than naught;
I walk the fields of quiet Arcadies,[3]
And wander by the brink of hoary seas,
Calmed to the tendance of untroubled thought;
Or if a livelier humor should enhance
The slow-time pulse, 'tis not for present strife,
The sordid zeal with which our age is rife,
Its mammon conflicts crowned by fraud or chance,
But gleamings of the lost, heroic life,
Flashed through the gorgeous vistas of romance.

AËTHRA[1]

IT is a sweet tradition, with a soul
Of tenderest pathos! Hearken, love! — for all
The sacred undercurrents of the heart
Thrill to its cordial music:
      Once a chief,
Philantus, king of Sparta, left the stern
And bleak defiles of his unfruitful land —
Girt by a band of eager colonists —

To seek new homes on fair Italian plains.[2]
Apollo's[3] oracle had darkly spoken:
" *Where'er from cloudless skies a plenteous shower*
Outpours, the Fates decree that ye should pause
And rear your household deities!"
                              Racked by doubt
Philantus traversed with his faithful band
Full many a bounteous realm; but still defeat
Darkened his banners, and the strong-walled towns
His desperate sieges grimly laughed to scorn!
Weighed down by anxious thoughts, one sultry eve
The warrior — his rude helmet cast aside —
Rested his weary head upon the lap
Of his fair wife, who loved him tenderly;
And there he drank a generous draught of sleep.
She, gazing on his brow, all worn with toil,
And his dark locks, which pain had silvered over
With glistening touches of a frosty rime,
Wept on the sudden bitterly; her tears
Fell on his face, and, wondering, he woke.
" O blest art thou, my Aëthra, *my clear sky*,"
He cried exultant, "from whose pitying blue
A heart-rain falls to fertilize my fate:
Lo! the deep riddle's solved — the gods spake truth!"

So the next night he stormed Tarentum,[4] took
The enemy's host at vantage, and o'erthrew
His mightiest captains. Thence with kindly sway
He ruled those pleasant regions he had won, —
But dearer even than his rich demesnes
The love of her whose gentle tears unlocked
The close-shut mystery of the Oracle!

UNDER THE PINE [1]

To the memory of Henry Timrod

THE same majestic pine is lifted high
  Against the twilight sky,
The same low, melancholy music grieves
  Amid the topmost leaves,[2]
As when I watched, and mused, and dreamed with
    him,
  Beneath these shadows dim.

O Tree! hast thou no memory at thy core
  Of one who comes no more?
No yearning memory of those scenes that were
  So richly calm and fair,
When the last rays of sunset, shimmering down,
  Flashed like a royal crown?

And he, with hand outstretched and eyes ablaze,
  Looked forth with burning[3] gaze,
And seemed to drink the sunset like strong wine,
  Or, hushed in trance divine,
Hailed the first shy and timorous glance from far
  Of evening's virgin star?

O Tree! against thy mighty trunk he laid
  His weary head; thy shade
Stole o'er him like the first cool spell of sleep:
  It brought a peace *so* deep
The unquiet passion died from out his eyes,
  As lightning from stilled skies.

And in that calm he loved to rest, and hear
  The soft wind-angels, clear
And sweet, among the uppermost branches sighing :
  Voices he heard replying
(Or so he dreamed) far up the mystic height,
  And pinions rustling light.

O Tree ! have not his poet-touch, his dreams
  So full of heavenly gleams,
Wrought through the folded dullness of thy bark,
  And all thy nature dark
Stirred to slow throbbings, and the fluttering fire
  Of faint, unknown desire ?

At least to me there sweeps no rugged ring
  That girds the forest king,
No immemorial stain, or awful rent
  (The mark of tempest spent),
No delicate leaf, no lithe bough, vine-o'ergrown,
  No distant, flickering cone,

But speaks of him, and seems to bring once more
  The joy, the love of yore ;
But most when breathed from out the sunset-land
  The sunset airs are bland,
That blow between the twilight and the night,
  Ere yet the stars are bright ;

For then that quiet eve comes back to me,
  When deeply, thrillingly,
He spake of lofty hopes which vanquish Death ;
  And on his mortal breath
A language of immortal meanings hung,
  That fired his heart and tongue.

For then unearthly breezes stir and sigh,
 Murmuring, " Look up! 'tis I :
Thy friend is near thee! Ah, thou canst not
  see! "
 And through the sacred tree
Passes what seems a wild and sentient thrill —
 Passes, and all is still! —

Still as the grave which holds his tranquil form,
 Hushed after many a storm, —
Still as the calm that crowns his marble brow,
 No pain can wrinkle now, —
Still as the peace — pathetic peace of God —
 That wraps the holy sod,

Where every flower from our dead minstrel's dust
 Should bloom, a type of trust, —
That faith which waxed to wings of heavenward
  might
 To bear his soul from night, —
That faith, dear Christ! whereby we pray to meet
 His spirit at God's feet!

CLOUD PICTURES [1]

HERE in these mellow grasses, the whole morn,
I love to rest; yonder, the ripening corn
Rustles its greenery; and his blithesome horn

Windeth the frolic breeze o'er field and dell,
Now pealing a bold stave with lusty swell,
Now falling to low breaths ineffable

Of whispered joyance.   At calm length I lie,
Fronting the broad blue spaces of the sky,
Covered with cloud-groups, softly journeying by :

An hundred shapes, fantastic, beauteous, strange,
Are theirs, as o'er yon airy waves they range
At the wind's will, from marvelous change to
    change ;

Castles, with guarded roof, and turret tall,
Great sloping archway, and majestic wall,
Sapped by the breezes to their noiseless fall !

Pagodas vague ! above whose towers outstream
Banners that wave with motions of a dream —
Rising, or drooping in the noontide gleam ;

Gray lines of Orient pilgrims : a gaunt band
On famished camels, o'er the desert sand
Plodding towards their prophet's Holy Land ;

Mid-ocean, — and a shoal of whales at play,
Lifting their monstrous frontlets to the day,
Thro' rainbow arches of sun-smitten spray ;

Followed by splintered icebergs, vast and lone,
Set in swift currents of some arctic zone,
Like fragments of a Titan's world o'erthrown ;

Next, measureless breadths of barren, treeless moor,
Whose vaporous verge fades down a glimmering
    shore,
Round which the foam-capped billows toss and
    roar !

Calms of bright water — like a fairy's wiles,
Wooing with ripply cadence and soft smiles,
The golden shore-slopes of Hesperian Isles;

Their inland plains rife with a rare increase
Of plumèd grain ! and many a snowy fleece
Shining athwart the dew-lit hills of peace;

Wrecks of gigantic cities — to the tune
Of some wise air-god built ! — o'er which the noon
Seems shuddering; caverns, such as the wan Moon

Shows in her desolate bosom; then, a crowd
Of awed and reverent faces, palely bowed
O'er a dead queen, laid in her ashy shroud —

A queen of eld — her pallid brow impearled
By gems barbaric ! her strange beauty furled
In mystic cerements of the antique world.

Weird pictures, fancy-gendered ! — one by one,
'Twixt blended beams and shadows, gold and dun,
These transient visions vanish in the sun.

LYRIC OF ACTION[1]

'Tis the part of a coward to brood
    O'er the past that is withered and dead:
What though the heart's roses are ashes and dust?
    What though the heart's music be fled?
    Still shine the grand heavens o'erhead,
Whence the voice of an angel thrills clear on the
        soul,
"Gird about thee thine armor, press on to the goal!"

If the faults or the crimes of thy youth
   Are a burden too heavy to bear,
What hope can re-bloom on the desolate waste
   Of a jealous and craven despair?
   Down, down with the fetters of fear!
In the strength of thy valor and manhood arise,
With the faith that illumes and the will that defies.

" *Too late!* " through God's infinite world,
   From his throne to life's nethermost fires,
" *Too late!* " is a phantom that flies at the dawn
   Of the soul that repents and aspires.
   If pure thou hast made thy desires,
There's no height the strong wings of immortals
      may gain
Which in striving to reach thou shalt strive for in
      vain.

Then, up to the contest with fate,
   Unbound by the past, which is dead!
What though the heart's roses are ashes and dust?
   What though the heart's music be fled?
   Still shine the fair heavens o'erhead;
And sublime as the seraph [2] who rules in the sun
Beams the promise of joy when the conflict is won!

SELECTIONS FROM HENRY TIMROD

TOO LONG, O SPIRIT OF STORM[1]

Too long, O Spirit of storm,
   Thy lightning sleeps in its sheath !
I am sick to the soul of yon pallid sky,
   And the moveless sea beneath.

Come down in thy strength on the deep !
   Worse dangers there are in life,
When the waves are still, and the skies look fair,
   Than in their wildest strife.

A friend I knew, whose days
   Were as calm as this sky overhead ;
But one blue morn that was fairest of all,
   The heart in his bosom fell dead.

And they thought him alive while he walked
   The streets that he walked in youth —
Ah ! little they guessed the seeming man
   Was a soulless corpse in sooth.

Come down in thy strength, O Storm !
   And lash the deep till it raves !
I am sick to the soul of that quiet sea,
   Which hides ten thousand graves.

A CRY TO ARMS [1]

Ho! woodsmen of the mountain side!
  Ho! dwellers in the vales!
Ho! ye who by the chafing tide
  Have roughened in the gales!
Leave barn and byre,[2] leave kin and cot,
  Lay by the bloodless spade;
Let desk, and case, and counter rot,
  And burn your books of trade.

The despot roves your fairest lands;
  And till he flies or fears,
Your fields must grow but armèd bands,
  Your sheaves be sheaves of spears!
Give up to mildew and to rust
  The useless tools of gain;
And feed your country's sacred dust
  With floods of crimson rain!

Come, with the weapons at your call —
  With musket, pike, or knife;
He wields the deadliest blade of all
  Who lightest holds his life.
The arm that drives its unbought blows
  With all a patriot's scorn,
Might brain a tyrant with a rose,
  Or stab him with a thorn.

Does any falter? let him turn
  To some brave maiden's eyes,
And catch the holy fires that burn
  In those sublunar skies.

Oh! could you like your women feel,
   And in their spirit march,
A day might see your lines of steel
   Beneath the victor's arch.

What hope, O God! would not grow warm
   When thoughts like these give cheer?
The Lily calmly braves the storm,
   And shall the Palm Tree fear?
No! rather let its branches court
   The rack [3] that sweeps the plain;
And from the Lily's regal port
   Learn how to breast the strain!

Ho! woodsmen of the mountain side!
   Ho! dwellers in the vales!
Ho! ye who by the roaring tide
   Have roughened in the gales!
Come! flocking gayly to the fight,
   From forest, hill, and lake;
We battle for our Country's right,
   And for the Lily's sake!

ODE [1]

I

SLEEP sweetly in your humble graves,
   Sleep, martyrs of a fallen cause;
Though yet no marble column craves
   The pilgrim here to pause.

II

In seeds of laurel in the earth
    The blossom of your fame is blown,
And somewhere, waiting for its birth,
    The shaft is in the stone! [2]

III

Meanwhile, behalf [3] the tardy years
    Which keep in trust your storied tombs,
Behold! your sisters bring their tears,
    And these memorial blooms.

IV

Small tributes! but your shades will smile
    More proudly on these wreaths to-day,
Than when some cannon-molded pile [4]
    Shall overlook this bay.

V

Stoop, angels, hither from the skies!
    There is no holier spot of ground
Than where defeated valor lies,
    By mourning beauty crowned.

FLOWER-LIFE [1]

I THINK that, next to your sweet eyes,
And pleasant books, and starry skies,
    I love the world of flowers;

Less for their beauty of a day,
Than for the tender things they say,
And for a creed I've held alway,
    That they are sentient powers.[2]

It may be matter for a smile —
And I laugh secretly the while
    I speak the fancy out —
But that they love, and that they woo,
And that they often marry too,
And do as noisier creatures do,
    I've not the faintest doubt.

And so, I cannot deem it right
To take them from the glad sunlight,
    As I have sometimes dared ;
Though not without an anxious sigh
Lest this should break some gentle tie,
Some covenant of friendship, I
    Had better far have spared.

And when, in wild or thoughtless hours,
My hand hath crushed the tiniest flowers,
    I ne'er could shut from sight
The corpses of the tender things,
With other drear imaginings,
And little angel-flowers with wings
    Would haunt me through the night.

Oh ! say you, friend, the creed is fraught
With sad, and even with painful thought,
    Nor could you bear to know

That such capacities belong
To creatures helpless against wrong,
At once too weak to fly the strong
    Or front the feeblest foe?

So be it always, then, with you;
So be it — whether false or true —
    I press my faith on none;
If other fancies please you more,
The flowers shall blossom as before,
Dear as the Sibyl-leaves [3] of yore,
    But senseless every one.

Yet, though I give you no reply,
It were not hard to justify
    My creed to partial ears;
But, conscious of the cruel part,
My rhymes would flow with faltering art,
I could not plead against your heart,
    Nor reason with your tears.

SONNET [1]

Poet! if on a lasting fame be bent
    Thy unperturbing hopes, thou wilt not roam
    Too far from thine own happy heart and home;
Cling to the lowly earth and be content!

So shall thy name be dear to many a heart;
    So shall the noblest truths by thee be taught;
    The flower and fruit of wholesome human
        thought
Bless the sweet labors of thy gentle art.

The brightest stars are nearest to the earth,
  And we may track the mighty sun above,
  Even by the shadow of a slender flower.
  Always, O bard, humility is power!
And thou mayest draw from matters of the hearth
  Truths wide as nations, and as deep as love.

SONNET

Most men know love but as a part of life;[2]
  They hide it in some corner of the breast,
  Even from themselves; and only when they
    rest
In the brief pauses of that daily strife,
Wherewith the world might else be not so rife,
  They draw it forth (as one draws forth a toy
  To soothe some ardent, kiss-exacting boy)
And hold it up to sister, child, or wife.

Ah me! why may not love and life be one?[3]
  Why walk we thus alone, when by our side,
  Love, like a visible God, might be our guide?
How would the marts grow noble! and the street,
Worn like a dungeon floor by weary feet,
Seem then a golden court-way of the Sun!

THE SUMMER BOWER[1]

It is a place whither I have often gone
For peace, and found it, secret, hushed, and cool,
A beautiful recess in neighboring woods.

Trees of the soberest hues, thick-leaved and tall,
Arch it o'erhead and column it around,
Framing a covert, natural and wild,
Domelike and dim; though nowhere so enclosed
But that the gentlest breezes reach the spot
Unwearied and unweakened.   Sound is here
A transient and unfrequent visitor;
Yet, if the day be calm, not often then,
Whilst the high pines in one another's arms
Sleep, you may sometimes with unstartled ear
Catch the far fall of voices, how remote
You know not, and you do not care to know.
The turf is soft and green, but not a flower
Lights the recess, save one, star-shaped and
      bright —
I do not know its name — which here and there
Gleams like a sapphire set in emerald.
A narrow opening in the branchèd roof,
A single one, is large enough to show,
With that half glimpse a dreamer loves so much,
The blue air and the blessing of the sky.
Thither I always bent my idle steps,
When griefs depressed, or joys disturbed my
      heart,
And found the calm I looked for, or returned
Strong with the quiet rapture in my soul.[2]
                              But one day,
One of those July days when winds have fled
One knows not whither, I, most sick in mind
With thoughts that shall be nameless, yet, no
      doubt,
Wrong, or at least unhealthful, since though dark

With gloom, and touched with discontent, they
    had
No adequate excuse, nor cause, nor end,
I, with these thoughts, and on this summer day,
Entered the accustomed haunt, and found for once
No medicinal virtue.

              Not a leaf
Stirred with the whispering welcome which I
    sought,
But in a close and humid atmosphere,
Every fair plant and implicated bough
Hung lax and lifeless.   Something in the place,
Its utter stillness, the unusual heat,
And some more secret influence, I thought,
Weighed on the sense like sin.   Above I saw,
Though not a cloud was visible in heaven,
The pallid sky look through a glazèd mist
Like a blue eye in death.

                  The change, perhaps,
Was natural enough; my jaundiced sight,
The weather, and the time explain it all:
Yet have I drawn a lesson from the spot,
And shrined it in these verses for my heart.
Thenceforth those tranquil precincts I have sought
Not less, and in all shades of various moods;
But always shun to desecrate the spot
By vain repinings, sickly sentiments,
Or inconclusive sorrows.   Nature, though
Pure as she was in Eden when her breath
Kissed the white brow of Eve, doth not refuse,
In her own way and with a just reserve,
To sympathize with human suffering; [3]

But for the pains, the fever, and the fret
Engendered of a weak, unquiet heart,
She hath no solace; and who seeks her when
These be the troubles over which he moans,
Reads in her unreplying lineaments
Rebukes, that, to the guilty consciousness,
Strike like contempt.

SELECTIONS FROM SIDNEY LANIER

SONG OF THE CHATTAHOOCHEE [1]

Out of the hills of Habersham,
   Down the valleys of Hall,[2]
The hurrying rain,[3] to reach the plain,
   Has run the rapid and leapt the fall,
Split at the rock and together again,
Accepted his bed, or narrow or wide,
And fled from folly on every side,
   With a lover's pain to attain the plain,
     Far from the hills of Habersham,
     Far from the valleys of Hall.

All down the hills of Habersham,
   All through the valleys of Hall,
The rushes cried, *Abide, abide ;*
   The wilful water weeds held me thrall,
The laurel, slow-laving,[4] turned my tide,
The ferns and the fondling grass said *stay,*
The dewberry dipped for to win delay,[5]
   And the little reeds sighed *Abide, abide,*
     Here in the hills of Habersham,
     Here in the valleys of Hall.

High over the hills of Habersham,
   Veiling the valleys of Hall,

The hickory told me manifold
    Fair tales of shade, the poplar tall
Wrought me her shadowy self to hold,
The chestnut, the oak, the walnut, the pine,
Overleaning, with flickering meaning and sign,
    Said, *Pass not so cold these manifold*
      Deep shades of the hills of Habersham,
      These glades in the valleys of Hall.

And oft in the hills of Habersham,
    And oft in the valleys of Hall,
The white quartz shone, and the smooth brook-
      stone
    Barred[6] me of passage with friendly brawl,
And many a metal lay sad, alone,
And the diamond, the garnet, the amethyst,
And the crystal that prisons a purple mist,
    Showed lights like my own from each cordial
      stone[7]
      In the clefts of the hills of Habersham,
      In the beds of the valleys of Hall.

But oh, not the hills of Habersham,
    And oh, not the valleys of Hall,
Shall hinder the rain from attaining the plain,[8]
    For downward the voices of duty call —
Downward to toil and be mixed with the main.
The dry fields burn and the mills are to turn,
And a thousand meadows[9] mortally yearn,
    And the final[10] main from beyond the plain
      Calls o'er the hills of Habersham,
      And calls through the valleys of Hall.

THE CRYSTAL [1]

At midnight, death's and truth's unlocking time,
When far within the spirit's hearing rolls
The great soft rumble of the course of things —
A bulk of silence in a mask of sound —
When darkness clears our vision that by day
Is sun-blind, and the soul's a ravening owl
For truth, and flitteth here and there about
Low-lying woody tracts of time and oft
Is minded for to sit upon a bough,
Dry-dead and sharp, of some long-stricken tree
And muse in that gaunt place, — 'twas then my
      heart,
Deep in the meditative dark, cried out:

Ye companies of governor-spirits grave,
Bards, and old bringers-down of flaming news
From steep-walled heavens, holy malcontents,
Sweet seers, and stellar visionaries, all
That brood about the skies of poesy,
Full bright ye shine, insuperable stars;
Yet, if a man look hard upon you, none
With total luster blazeth, no, not one
But hath some heinous freckle of the flesh
Upon his shining cheek, not one but winks
His ray, opaqued with intermittent mist
Of defect; yea, you masters all must ask
Some sweet forgiveness, which we leap to give,
We lovers of you, heavenly-glad to meet
Your largess so with love, and interplight
Your geniuses with our mortalities.

Thus unto thee, O sweetest Shakspere sole,[2]
A hundred hurts a day I do forgive
('Tis little, but, enchantment! 'tis for thee):
Small curious quibble; . . . Henry's fustian roar
Which frights away that sleep he invocates;[3]
Wronged Valentine's[4] unnatural haste to yield;
Too-silly shifts of maids that mask as men
In faint disguises that could ne'er disguise —
Viola, Julia, Portia, Rosalind;[5]
Fatigues most drear, and needless overtax
Of speech obscure that had as lief be plain.

     . . . Father Homer, thee,
Thee also I forgive thy sandy wastes
Of prose and catalogue,[6] thy drear harangues
That tease the patience of the centuries,
Thy sleazy scrap of story, — but a rogue's
Rape of a light-o'-love,[7] — too soiled a patch
To broider with the gods.

     Thee, Socrates,[8]
Thou dear and very strong one, I forgive
Thy year-worn cloak, thine iron stringencies
That were but dandy upside-down,[9] thy words
Of truth that, mildlier spoke, had manlier wrought.

So, Buddha,[10] beautiful! I pardon thee
That all the All thou hadst for needy man
Was Nothing, and thy Best of being was
But not to be.

     Worn Dante,[11] I forgive
The implacable hates that in thy horrid hells

Or burn or freeze thy fellows, never loosed
By death, nor time, nor love.

                    And I forgive
Thee, Milton, those thy comic-dreadful wars [12]
Where, armed with gross and inconclusive steel,
Immortals smite immortals mortalwise,
And fill all heaven with folly.

                    Also thee,
Brave Æschylus,[13] thee I forgive, for that
Thine eye, by bare bright justice basilisked,
Turned not, nor ever learned to look where Love
Stands shining.

                So, unto thee, Lucretius [14] mine,
(For oh, what heart hath loved thee like to this
That's now complaining?) freely I forgive
Thy logic poor, thine error rich, thine earth
Whose graves eat souls and all.

                   Yea, all you hearts
Of beauty, and sweet righteous lovers large:
Aurelius [15] fine, oft superfine; mild Saint
A Kempis,[16] overmild; Epictetus,[17]
Whiles low in thought, still with old slavery tinct;
Rapt Behmen,[18] rapt too far; high Swedenborg,[19]
O'ertoppling; Langley,[20] that with but a touch
Of art hadst sung Piers Plowman to the top
Of English songs, whereof 'tis dearest, now,
And most adorable; Cædmon,[21] in the morn
A-calling angels with the cowherd's call
That late brought up the cattle; Emerson,
Most wise, that yet, in finding Wisdom, lost

Thy Self, sometimes; tense Keats, with angels'
    nerves
Where men's were better; Tennyson, largest voice
Since Milton, yet some register of wit
Wanting, — all, all, I pardon, ere 'tis asked,
Your more or less, your little mole that marks
Your brother and your kinship seals to man.
But Thee, but Thee, O sovereign Seer of time,
But Thee, O poets' Poet, Wisdom's Tongue,
But Thee, O man's best Man, O love's best Love,
O perfect life in perfect labor writ,
O all men's Comrade, Servant, King, or Priest, —
What *if* or *yet*, what mole, what flaw, what lapse,
What least defect or shadow of defect,
What rumor, tattled by an enemy,
Of inference loose, what lack of grace
Even in torture's grasp, or sleep's, or death's, —
Oh, what amiss may I forgive in Thee,
Jesus, good Paragon, thou Crystal Christ? [22]

SUNRISE [1]

In my sleep I was fain of their fellowship, fain
Of the live-oak, the marsh, and the main.
The little green leaves would not let me alone in
    my sleep;
Up breathed from the marshes, a message of range
    and of sweep,
Interwoven with waftures of wild sea-liberties, drift-
    ing,
Came through the lapped leaves sifting, sifting,
        Came to the gates of sleep.

Then my thoughts, in the dark of the dungeon-keep
Of the Castle of Captives hid in the City of Sleep,
Upstarted, by twos and by threes assembling:
The gates of sleep fell a-trembling
Like as the lips of a lady that forth falter *yes*,
   Shaken with happiness:
   The gates of sleep stood wide.

I have waked, I have come, my beloved! I might
  not abide:
I have come ere the dawn, O beloved, my live-oaks,
  to hide
   In your gospeling glooms,[2] — to be
As a lover in heaven, the marsh my marsh and the
  sea my sea.

Tell me, sweet burly-barked, man-bodied Tree
That mine arms in the dark are embracing, dost
  know
From what fount are these tears at thy feet which
  flow?
They rise not from reason, but deeper inconsequent
  deeps.
   Reason's not one that weeps.
   What logic of greeting lies
Betwixt dear over-beautiful trees and the rain of
  the eyes?

O cunning green leaves, little masters! like as ye
  gloss
All the dull-tissued dark with your luminous darks
  that emboss

The vague blackness of night into pattern and plan,
> So,
(But would I could know, but would I could know,)
With your question embroid'ring the dark of the
> question of man, —
So, with your silences purfling this silence of man
While his cry to the dead for some knowledge is
> under the ban,
>> Under the ban, —
>> So, ye have wrought me
Designs on the night of our knowledge, — yea, ye
> have taught me,
>> So,
That haply we know somewhat more than we
> know.

> Ye lispers, whisperers, singers in storms,
> Ye consciences murmuring faiths under forms,
> Ye ministers meet for each passion that grieves,
> Friendly, sisterly, sweetheart leaves,[3]
Oh, rain me down from your darks that contain
> me
Wisdoms ye winnow from winds that pain me, —
Sift down tremors of sweet-within-sweet
That advise me of more than they bring, — repeat
Me the woods-smell that swiftly but now brought
> breath
From the heaven-side bank of the river of death, —
Teach me the terms of silence, — preach me
The passion of patience, — sift me, — impeach
> me, —

And there, oh there
As ye hang with your myriad palms upturned in
      the air,
            Pray me a myriad prayer.[4]

My gossip, the owl, — is it thou
That out of the leaves of the low-hanging bough,
As I pass to the beach, art stirred?
Dumb woods, have ye uttered a bird?

Reverend Marsh, low-couched along the sea,
Old chemist, rapt in alchemy,
            Distilling silence, — lo,
That which our father-age had died to know —
The menstruum that dissolves all matter — thou
Hast found it : for this silence, filling now
The globèd clarity of receiving space,
This solves us all : man, matter, doubt, disgrace,
Death, love, sin, sanity,
Must in yon silence' clear solution lie.
Too clear!   That crystal nothing who'll peruse?
The blackest night could bring us brighter news.
Yet precious qualities of silence haunt
Round these vast margins, ministrant.
Oh, if thy soul's at latter gasp for space,
With trying to breathe no bigger than thy race
Just to be fellowed, when that thou hast found
No man with room, or grace enough of bound
To entertain that New thou tell'st, thou art, —
'Tis here, 'tis here, thou canst unhand thy heart
And breathe it free, and breathe it free,
By rangy marsh, in lone sea-liberty.

The tide's at full: the marsh with flooded streams
Glimmers, a limpid labyrinth of dreams.
Each winding creek in grave entrancement lies
A rhapsody of morning-stars.   The skies
Shine scant with one forked galaxy, —
The marsh brags ten: looped on his breast they lie.

Oh, what if a sound should be made!
Oh, what if a bound should be laid
To this bow-and-string tension of beauty and
    silence a-spring, —
To the bend of beauty the bow, or the hold of
    silence the string!
I fear me, I fear me yon dome of diaphanous gleam
Will break as a bubble o'erblown in a dream, —
Yon dome of too-tenuous tissues of space and of
    night,
Overweighted with stars, overfreighted with light,
Oversated with beauty and silence, will seem
              But a bubble that broke in a dream,
If a bound of degree to this grace be laid,
              Or a sound or a motion made.

But no: it is made: list! somewhere, — mystery,
    where?
              In the leaves? in the air?
In my heart? is a motion made:
'Tis a motion of dawn, like a flicker of shade on
    shade.
In the leaves 'tis palpable: low multitudinous stir-
    ring

Upwinds through the woods; the little ones, softly
    conferring,
Have settled my lord's to be looked for; so; they
    are still;
But the air and my heart and the earth are
    a-thrill, —
And look where the wild duck sails round the bend
    of the river, —
        And look where a passionate shiver
        Expectant is bending the blades
Of the marsh-grass in serial shimmers and
    shades, —
And invisible wings, fast fleeting, fast fleeting,
        Are beating
The dark overhead as my heart beats, — and
    steady and free
Is the ebb-tide flowing from marsh to sea —
        (Run home, little streams,
        With your lapfuls of stars and dreams), —
And a sailor unseen is hoisting a-peak,
For list, down the inshore curve of the creek
        How merrily flutters the sail, —
And lo, in the East! Will the East unveil?
The East is unveiled, the East hath confessed
A flush: 'tis dead; 'tis alive; 'tis dead, ere the
    West
Was aware of it: nay, 'tis abiding, 'tis withdrawn:
Have a care, sweet Heaven! 'Tis Dawn.

Now a dream of a flame through that dream of a
    flush is uprolled:
To the zenith ascending, a dome of undazzling gold

Is builded, in shape as a beehive, from out of the
     sea :
The hive is of gold undazzling, but oh, the Bee,
The star-fed Bee, the build-fire Bee,
Of dazzling gold is the great Sun-Bee
That shall flash from the hive-hole over the sea.[5]
Yet now the dewdrop, now the morning gray,
Shall live their little lucid sober day
Ere with the sun their souls exhale away.
Now in each pettiest personal sphere of dew
The summ'd morn shines complete as in the blue
Big dewdrop of all heaven : with these lit shrines
O'er-silvered to the farthest sea-confines,
The sacramental marsh one pious plain
Of worship lies.   Peace to the ante-reign
Of Mary Morning, blissful mother mild,
Minded of nought but peace, and of a child.

Not slower than Majesty moves, for a mean and a
     measure
Of   motion, — not faster than dateless Olympian
     leisure [6]
Might pace with unblown ample garments from
     pleasure to pleasure, —
The wave-serrate sea-rim sinks unjarring, unreeling,
Forever revealing, revealing, revealing,
Edgewise, bladewise, halfwise, wholewise, — 'tis
     done !
          Good-morrow, lord Sun !
With several voice, with ascription one,
The woods and the marsh and the sea and my soul

Unto thee, whence the glittering stream of all
    morrows doth roll,
Cry good and past-good and most heavenly morrow,
    lord Sun.

O Artisan born in the purple, — Workman Heat, —
Parter of passionate atoms that travail to meet
And be mixed in the death-cold oneness, — inner-
    most Guest
At the marriage of elements, — fellow of publicans,
    — blest
King in the blouse of flame, that loiterest o'er
The idle skies, yet laborest fast evermore, —
Thou in the fine forge-thunder, thou, in the beat
Of the heart of a man, thou Motive, — Laborer
    Heat:
Yea, Artist, thou, of whose art yon sea's all news,
With his inshore greens and manifold mid-sea
    blues,
Pearl-glint, shell-tint, ancientest perfectest hues,
Ever shaming the maidens, — lily and rose
Confess thee, and each mild flame that glows
In the clarified virginal bosoms of stones that
    shine,
                It is thine, it is thine:

Thou chemist of storms, whether driving the winds
    a-swirl
Or a-flicker the subtiler essences polar that whirl
In the magnet earth, — yea, thou with a storm for
    a heart,
Rent with debate, many-spotted with question, part

From part oft sundered, yet ever a globèd light,
Yet ever the artist, ever more large and bright
Than the eye of a man may avail of : — manifold
  One,
I must pass from thy face, I must pass from the
  face of the Sun :

Old Want is awake and agog, every wrinkle
  a-frown ;
The worker must pass to his work in the terrible
  town :
But I fear not, nay, and I fear not the thing to be
  done ;
I am strong with the strength of my lord the
  Sun :
How dark, how dark soever the race that must
  needs be run,
    I am lit with the Sun.

Oh, never the mast-high run of the seas
  Of traffic shall hide thee,
Never the hell-colored smoke of the factories
    Hide thee,
Never the reek of the time's fen-politics
    Hide thee,
And ever my heart through the night shall with
  knowledge abide thee,
And ever by day shall my spirit, as one that hath
  tried thee,
Labor, at leisure, in art, — till yonder beside thee
    My soul shall float, friend Sun,
    The day being done.

SELECTIONS FROM FATHER RYAN

SONG OF THE MYSTIC [1]

I WALK down the Valley of Silence [2] —
  Down the dim, voiceless valley — alone!
And I hear not the fall of a footstep
  Around me, save God's and my own;
And the hush of my heart is as holy
  As hovers where angels have flown!

Long ago was I weary of voices
  Whose music my heart could not win;
Long ago was I weary of noises
  That fretted my soul with their din;
Long ago was I weary of places
  Where I met but the human — and sin. [3]

I walked in the world with the worldly;
  I craved what the world never gave;
And I said: "In the world each Ideal,
  That shines like a star on life's wave,
Is wrecked on the shores of the Real,
  And sleeps like a dream in a grave.

And still did I pine for the Perfect,
  And still found the False with the True;
I sought 'mid the Human for Heaven,

But caught a mere glimpse of its Blue :
And I wept when the clouds of the Mortal
    Veiled even that glimpse from my view.

And I toiled on, heart-tired of the Human,
    And I moaned 'mid the mazes of men,
Till I knelt, long ago, at an altar,
    And I heard a voice call me.   Since then
I walked down the Valley of Silence
    That lies far beyond mortal ken.

Do you ask what I found in the Valley ?
    'Tis my Trysting Place with the Divine.
And I fell at the feet of the Holy,
    And above me a voice said : " Be Mine."
And there arose from the depths of my spirit
    An echo — " My heart shall be thine."

Do you ask how I live in the Valley ?
    I weep — and I dream — and I pray.
But my tears are as sweet as the dewdrops
    That fall on the roses in May ;
And my prayer like a perfume from censers,
    Ascendeth to God night and day.

In the hush of the Valley of Silence
    I dream all the songs that I sing ;[4]
And the music floats down the dim Valley,
    Till each finds a word for a wing,
That to hearts, like the dove of the deluge
    A message of peace they may bring.

But far on the deep there are billows
  That never shall break on the beach;
And I have heard songs in the Silence
  That never shall float into speech;
And I have had dreams in the Valley
  Too lofty for language to reach.

And I have seen thoughts in the Valley —
  Ah me! how my spirit was stirred!
And they wear holy veils on their faces,
  Their footsteps can scarcely be heard:
They pass through the Valley like virgins,
  Too pure for the touch of a word! [5]

Do you ask me the place of the Valley,
  Ye hearts that are harrowed by care?
It lieth afar between mountains,
  And God and His angels are there:
And one is the dark mount of Sorrow,
  And one the bright mountain of Prayer.

THE CONQUERED BANNER [1]

Furl that Banner, for 'tis weary;
Round its staff 'tis drooping dreary;
  Furl it, fold it, it is best;
For there's not a man to wave it,
And there's not a sword to save it,
And there's not one left to lave it
In the blood which heroes gave it;
And its foes now scorn and brave it;
  Furl it, hide it — let it rest! [2]

Take that Banner down! 'tis tattered;
Broken is its staff and shattered;
And the valiant hosts are scattered
    Over whom it floated high.
Oh! 'tis hard for us to fold it;
Hard to think there's none to hold it;
Hard that those who once unrolled it
    Now must furl it with a sigh.

Furl that Banner! furl it sadly!
Once ten thousands hailed it gladly,
And ten thousands wildly, madly,
    Swore it should forever wave;
Swore that foeman's sword should never
Hearts like theirs entwined dissever,
Till that flag should float forever
    O'er their freedom or their grave!

Furl it! for the hands that grasped it,
And the hearts that fondly clasped it,
    Cold and dead are lying low;
And that Banner — it is trailing!
While around it sounds the wailing
    Of its people in their woe.

For, though conquered, they adore it!
Love the cold, dead hands that bore it!
Weep for those who fell before it!
Pardon those who trailed and tore it![3]
But, oh! wildly they deplore it,
    Now who furl and fold it so.

Furl that Banner!   True, 'tis gory,
Yet 'tis wreathed around with glory,
And 'twill live in song and story,
    Though its folds are in the dust:
For its fame on brightest pages,
Penned by poets and by sages,
Shall go sounding down the ages —
    Furl its folds though now we must.

Furl that Banner, softly, slowly!
Treat it gently — it is holy —
    For it droops above the dead.
Touch it not — unfold it never,
Let it droop there, furled forever,
    For its people's hopes are dead! [4]

THE SWORD OF ROBERT LEE [1]

FORTH from its scabbard, pure and bright,
    Flashed the sword of Lee!
Far in the front of the deadly fight,
High o'er the brave in the cause of Right,
Its stainless sheen, like a beacon light,
    Led us to victory.

Out of its scabbard, where full long
    It slumbered peacefully,
Roused from its rest by the battle's song,
Shielding the feeble, smiting the strong,
Guarding the right, avenging the wrong,
    Gleamed the sword of Lee.

Forth from its scabbard, high in air
    Beneath Virginia's sky —
And they who saw it gleaming there,
And knew who bore it, knelt to swear
That where that sword led they would dare
    To follow — and to die.

Out of its scabbard!   Never hand
    Waved sword from stain as free;
Nor purer sword led braver band,
Nor braver bled for a brighter land,
Nor brighter land had a cause so grand,
    Nor cause a chief like Lee![2]

Forth from its scabbard !   How we prayed
    That sword might victor be;
And when our triumph was delayed,
And many a heart grew sore afraid,
We still hoped on while gleamed the blade
    Of noble Robert Lee.

Forth from its scabbard all in vain
    Bright flashed the sword of Lee;
'Tis shrouded now in its sheath again,
It sleeps the sleep of our noble slain,
Defeated, yet without a stain,
    Proudly and peacefully.

DEATH [1]

Out of the shadows of sadness,
    Into the sunshine of gladness,
        Into the light of the blest;

Out of a land very dreary,
Out of the world very weary,
  Into the rapture of rest.

Out of to-day's sin and sorrow,
Into a blissful to-morrow,
  Into a day without gloom ;
Out of a land filled with sighing,
Land of the dead and the dying,
  Into a land without tomb.

Out of a life of commotion,
Tempest-swept oft as the ocean,
  Dark with the wrecks drifting o'er,
Into a land calm and quiet;
Never a storm cometh nigh it,
  Never a wreck on its shore.

Out of a land in whose bowers
Perish and fade all the flowers;
  Out of the land of decay,
Into the Eden where fairest
Of flowerets, and sweetest and rarest,
  Never shall wither away.

Out of the world of the wailing
Thronged with the anguished and ailing;
  Out of the world of the sad,
Into the world that rejoices —
World of bright visions and voices —
  Into the world of the glad.

Out of a life ever mournful,
Out of a land very lornful,
  Where in bleak exile we roam,[2]
Into a joy-land above us,
Where there's a Father to love us —
  Into our home — " Sweet Home."

PRESENTIMENT [1]

COMETH a voice from a far-land,
  Beautiful, sad, and low ;
Shineth a light from the star-land
  Down on the night of my woe ;
And a white hand, with a garland,
  Biddeth my spirit to go.

Away and afar from the night-land,
  Where sorrow o'ershadows my way,
To the splendors and skies of the light-land,
  Where reigneth eternity's day, —
To the cloudless and shadowless bright-land,
  Whose sun never passeth away.

And I knew the voice ; not a sweeter
  On earth or in Heaven can be ;
And never did shadow pass fleeter
  Than it, and its strange melody ;
And I know I must hasten to meet her,
  " Yea, *Sister !* Thou callest to me ! "

And I saw the light; 'twas not seeming,
  It flashed from the crown that she wore,
And the brow, that with jewels was gleaming,
  My lips had kissed often of yore!
And the eyes, that with rapture were beaming,
  Had smiled on me sweetly before.

And I saw the hand with the garland,
  Ethel's hand — holy and fair;
Who went long ago to the far-land
  To weave me the wreath I shall wear;
And to-night I look up to the star-land
  And pray that I soon may be there. [2]

NIGHT THOUGHTS

Some reckon their age by years,
  Some measure their life by art, —
But some tell their days by the flow of their tears,
  And their life, by the moans of their heart.

The dials of earth may show
  The length — not the depth of years;
Few or many they come, few or many they go,
  But our time is best measured by tears.

Ah! not by the silver gray
  That creeps through the sunny hair,
And not by the scenes that we pass on our way,
  And not by the furrows the fingers of care,

On forehead and face, have made :
   Not so do we count our years ;
Not by the sun of the earth, but the shade
   Of our souls, and the fall of our tears.

For the young are oft-times old,
   Though their brow be bright and fair ;
While their blood beats warm, their heart lies cold —
   O'er them the springtime, but winter is there.

And the old are oft-times young,
   When their hair is thin and white ;
And they sing in age, as in youth they sung,
   And they laugh, for their cross was light.

But bead by bead I tell
   The rosary of my years ;
From a cross to a cross they lead, — 'tis well !
   And they're blest with a blessing of tears.

Better a day of strife
   Than a century of sleep ;
Give me instead of a long stream of life,
   The tempests and tears of the deep.

A thousand joys may foam
   On the billows of all the years ;
But never the foam brings the brave [2] heart home —
   It reaches the haven through tears.

NOTES TO SELECTIONS

THE STAR-SPANGLED BANNER

1. For a brief statement of the circumstances that gave rise to the poem, see sketch of Key, page 12.

2. Fort McHenry, on the north bank of the Patapsco, below Baltimore, was attacked by the British fleet, September 13, 1814.

3. The attack being unsuccessful, the British became disheartened and withdrew.

4. Before the attack upon Baltimore, the British had taken Washington and burned the capitol and other public buildings.

With this poem may be compared other martial lyrics, such as Hopkinson's *Hail Columbia*, Mrs. Howe's *Battle Hymn of the Republic*, Campbell's *Ye Mariners of England* and *Battle of the Baltic*, Tennyson's *Charge of the Light Brigade*, etc.

STANZAS

1. See sketch of Wilde, page 13. This song was translated into Greek by Anthony Barclay and announced as a newly discovered ode by Alcæus. The trick, however, was soon detected by scholars, and the author of the poem received a due meed of praise.

2. The brevity of life has been a favorite theme of poets ever since Job (vii. 6) declared, " Our days are swifter than a weaver's shuttle."

3. The reference seems to be to the shore about the Bay of Tampa on the west coast of Florida.

A FAREWELL TO AMERICA

1. See page 13

2. It will be remembered that the poet was a native of Ireland.

3. The years 1834–1840 were spent in Europe, chiefly in Italy.

Compare with this Byron's farewell to England, in Canto 1 of *Childe Harold*.

THE CLOSING YEAR

1. See sketch of Prentice, page 14. The flight of time is another favorite theme with poets. *The Closing Year* should be compared with Bryant's *The Flood of Years*; similar in theme, the two poems have much in common. The closing lines of Bryant's poem express a sweet faith that relieves the somber tone of the preceding reflections : —

> " In the room
> Of this grief-shadowed present, there shall be
> A Present in whose reign no grief shall gnaw
> The heart, and never shall a tender tie
> Be broken; in whose reign the eternal Change
> That waits on growth and action shall proceed
> With everlasting Concord hand in hand."

2. This is a reference to the belief that one of the seven stars originally supposed to form the Pleiades has disappeared. Such a phenomenon is not unknown ; modern astronomers record several such disappearances. See Simms's *The Lost Pleiad*, following.

THE LOST PLEIAD

1. See note above. There is a peculiar fitness in the reference to the sea in this poem; for the constellation of the Pleiades was named by the Greeks from their word *plein*, to sail, because the Mediterranean was navigable with safety during the months these stars were visible.

2. The poet seems to associate the Chaldean shepherd with the Magi, who, as astrologers, observed the stars with profound interest. The hope expressed for the return of the star cannot be regarded, in the light of modern astronomy, as entirely fanciful. Only recently a new star has flamed forth in the constellation Perseus.

3. The fixed stars, continually giving forth immeasurable quantities of heat, are in a process of cooling. Sooner or later they will become dark bodies. Astronomers tell us that there is reason to believe that the dark bodies or burned-out suns of the universe are more numerous than the bright ones, though the number of the latter exceeds 125 millions. The existence of such dark bodies has been established beyond a reasonable doubt.

4. A reference to the old belief that the stars make music in their courses. In Job (xxxviii. 7) we read: "When the morning stars sang together." According to the Platonic philosophy, this music of the spheres, too faint for mortal ears, was heard only by the gods. Shakespeare has given beautiful expression to this belief:—

> "There's not the smallest orb which thou behold'st
> But in his motion like an angel sings,
> Still quiring to the young-eyed cherubins;
> Such harmony is in immortal souls;
> But whilst this muddy vesture of decay
> Doth grossly close it in, we cannot hear it."
> — *Merchant of Venice*, Act V., Sc. 1.

THE SWAMP FOX

1. See sketch of Simms, page 16. This poem is found in *The Partisan*, the first of three novels descriptive of the Revolution. Read a biographical sketch of General Francis Marion (1732–1795), whose shrewdness in attack and escape earned for him the *sobriquet* "Swamp Fox."

2. Sir Banastre Tarleton (1754–1833) was a lieutenant colonel in the army of Cornwallis. He was a brilliant and successful officer, but was defeated by General Morgan in the battle of Cowpens in 1781.

3. "Sumter, Marion, and other South Carolina leaders found places of refuge in the great swamps which are found in parts of the state; and from these they kept up an active warfare with the British. Their desperate battles, night marches, surprises, and hairbreadth escapes make this the most exciting and interesting period of the Revolution." — Johnston's *History of the United States*.

4. Marion's principal field of operations lay between the Santee and Pedee rivers.

5. Marion held the rank of captain at the outbreak of the Revolution, and was made lieutenant colonel for gallant conduct in the defence of Fort Moultrie, June 28, 1776. Later he was made general.

6. A water tortoise or snapping turtle.

Compare Bryant's *Song of Marion's Men*.

A HEALTH

1. See sketch of Pinkney, page 18. The flowing or lilting melody of this and the following songs is quite remarkable. It is traceable to the skillful use of liquid consonants and short vowels, and the avoidance of harsh consonant combinations.

2. The irregularities of this stanza are remarkable. The middle rhyme used in the first and seventh lines of the other stanzas is here lacking. It seems to have been an oversight on the part of the poet.

3. With this drinking song we may compare the well-known one of Ben Jonson: —

> " Drink to me only with thine eyes,
>   And I will pledge with mine;
> Or leave a kiss but in the cup,
>   And I'll not look for wine.
> The thirst that from the soul doth rise
>   Doth ask a drink divine;
> But might I of Jove's nectar sup,
>   I would not change for thine.
>
> " I sent thee late a rosy wreath,
>   Not so much honoring thee
> As giving it a hope that there
>   It could not withered be;

> But thou thereon didst only breathe
>   And sent'st it back to me;
> Since when it grows, and smells, **I swear,**
>   Not of itself, but thee."

SONG

1. This same simile occurs in a beautiful poem by Amelia
C. Welby (1819–1852), a Southern poet of no mean gifts, entitled *Twilight at Sea* : —

> " The twilight hours like birds flew by,
>   As lightly and as free;
> Ten thousand stars were in the sky,
>   Ten thousand on the sea;
> For every wave with dimpled face,
>   That leaped upon the air,
> Had caught a star in its embrace,
>   And held it trembling there."

FLORENCE VANE

1. See sketch of Cooke, page 19. In the preface to the
volume from which this poem is taken, the author tells us that
Florence Vane and *Rosalie Lee*, another brief lyric, had " met
with more favor than I could ever perceive their just claim
to." Hence he was kept from " venturing upon the correction
of some faults." *Rosalie Lee* is more than usually defective
in meter and rhyme, but *Florence Vane* cannot easily be im-
proved.

2. " My meaning, I suppose," the poet wrote an inquiring
friend, " was that Florence did not want the capacity to love,
but directed her love to no object. Her passions went flowing like a lost river. Byron has a kindred idea expressed by
the same figure. Perhaps his verses were in my mind when
I wrote my own : —

> " ' She was the ocean to the river of his thoughts,
>   Which terminated all.' — *The Dream.*

But no verse ought to require to be interpreted, and if I were
composing Florence Vane now, I would avoid the over con-
centrated expression in the two lines, and make the idea
clearer." — *Southern Literary Messenger*, 1850, p. 370.

THE BIVOUAC OF THE DEAD

1. See sketch of O'Hara, page 21, for the occasion of this poem.

2. The American force numbered 4769 men; the Mexican force under Santa Anna, 21,000. The latter was confident of victory, and sent a flag of truce to demand surrender. "You are surrounded by 20,000 men," wrote the Mexican general, "and cannot, in any human probability, avoid suffering a rout, and being cut to pieces with your troops." Gen. Taylor replied, "I beg leave to say that I decline acceding to your request."

3. The battle raged for ten hours with varying success. There was great determination on both sides, as is shown by the heavy losses. The Americans lost 267 killed and 456 wounded; Santa Anna stated his loss at 1500, which was probably an underestimate. He left 500 dead on the field. The battle was a decisive one, and left northeastern Mexico in the hands of the Americans.

4. The reference is to Zachary Taylor, who was in command of the American forces. Though born in Virginia, he was brought up in Kentucky, and won his first laurels in command of Kentuckians in the War of 1812, during which he was engaged in fighting the Indian allies of Great Britain. His victory at Buena Vista aroused great enthusiasm in the United States, and more than any other event led to his election as President.

5. The plateau on which the battle was fought, so called from the mountain pass of Angostura (the narrows) leading to it from the South.

6. Kentucky is here beautifully likened to a Spartan mother who was accustomed to say, as she handed a shield to her son departing for war, "Come back with this or upon this."

THE VIRGINIANS OF THE VALLEY

1. See sketch of Ticknor, page 22, for the occasion of this poem. In this poem the exact meaning and sequence of thought do not appear till after repeated readings.

2. Alexander Spotswood (1676–1740) was governor of Virginia 1710–1723. He led an exploring expedition across the Blue Ridge and took possession of the Valley of Virginia "in the name of his Majesty King George of England." On his return to Williamsburg he presented to each of his companions a miniature golden horseshoe to be worn upon the breast. Those who took part in the expedition, which was then regarded as a formidable undertaking, were subsequently known as the "Knights of the Golden Horseshoe."

3. "The Old Dominion" is a popular name for Virginia. Its origin may be traced to acts of Parliament, in which it is designated as "the colony and dominion of Virginia." In his *History of Virginia* (1629) Captain John Smith calls this colony and dominion *Old Virginia* in contradistinction to *New England*.

LITTLE GIFFEN

1. See page 23. Of this poem Maurice Thompson said: "If there is a finer lyric than this in the whole realm of poetry, I should be glad to read it."

2. Probably the battle of Murfreesboro, which opened December 31, 1862, and lasted three days. Union loss 14,000; Confederate, 11,000.

3. He was killed in some battle near Atlanta early in 1864.

4. A reference to King Arthur and the Knights of the Round Table.

With this poem should be compared Browning's *Incident of the French Camp*.

MUSIC IN CAMP

1. See sketch of John R. Thompson, page 23.

2. The incident on which the poem is based may have occurred in 1862 or 1863. In both years the Union and Confederate forces occupied opposite banks of the Rappahannock.

A NOVEMBER NOCTURNE

1. See sketch of Mrs. Preston, page 25. This and the following poem are good examples of her poetic art, and

exhibit, at the same time, her reflective religious temperament.

2. *Resurgam* (Latin), I shall rise again.

CALLING THE ANGELS IN

1. "And Abraham sat in the tent door in the heat of the day; and he lifted up his eyes and looked, and, lo, three men stood by him: and when he saw them, he ran to meet them from the tent door, and bowed himself toward the ground, and said, My Lord, if now I have found favour in thy sight, pass not away, I pray thee, from thy servant." — *Genesis* xviii. 1–3.

NOTES TO SELECTIONS FROM POE

For a general introduction to the selections from Poe, the biographical and critical sketch in Chap. II should be read.

TO HELEN

1. This was Mrs. Helen Stannard, the mother of one of Poe's schoolmates in Richmond. Her kind and gracious manner made a deep impression on his boyish heart, and soothed his passionate, turbulent nature. In after years this poem was inspired, as the poet tells us, by the memory of "the one idolatrous and purely ideal love" of his restless youth.

2. The reference seems to be to the ancient Ligurian town of Nicæa, now Nice, in France. The "perfumed sea" would then be the Ligurian sea. But one half suspects that it was the scholarly and musical sound of the word, rather than any aptness of classical reference, that led to the use of the word "Nicæan."

3. This appears to be Poe's indefinite and poetic way of saying that the lady's beauty and grace brought him an uplifting sense of happiness. After seeing her the first time, "He returned home in a dream, with but one thought, one hope in life — to hear again the sweet and gracious words that had made the desolate world so beautiful to him, and filled his lonely heart with the oppression of a new joy." — Ingram's *Edgar Allan Poe*, Vol. I, p. 32.

4. Psyche was represented as so exquisitely beautiful that mortals did not dare to love, but only to worship her. The poet could pay no higher tribute to "Helen."

This little poem — very beautiful in itself — illustrates Poe's characteristics as a poet : it is indefinite, musical, and intense.

ANNABEL LEE

1. This poem is a tribute to his wife, to whom his beautiful devotion has already been spoken of. "I believe," says Mrs. Osgood, "she was the only woman whom he ever truly loved; and this is evidenced by the exquisite pathos of the little poem lately written, called 'Annabel Lee,' of which she was the subject, and which is by far the most natural, simple, tender, and touchingly beautiful of all his songs."

2. This is Poe's poetic designation of America.

3. "Virginia Clemm, born on the 13th of August, 1822, was still a child when her handsome cousin Edgar revisited Baltimore after his escapade at West Point. A more than cousinly affection, which gradually grew in intensity, resulted from their frequent communion, and ultimately, whilst one, at least, of the two cousins was but a child, they were married." — Ingram's *Edgar Allan Poe*, Vol. I, p. 136.

4. These were the angels, to whom "Annabel Lee" was akin in sweet, gentle character. "A lady angelically beautiful in person, and not less beautiful in spirit." — Captain Mayne Reid.

5. This may be literally true. At all events, it is related that he visited the tomb of "Helen"; and "when the autumnal rains fell, and the winds wailed mournfully over the graves, he lingered longest, and came away most regretfully."

THE HAUNTED PALACE

1. This admirable poem is an allegory. The "stately palace" is a man who after a time loses his reason. With this fact in mind, the poem becomes quite clear. The "banners yellow, glorious, golden" is the hair; the "luminous windows" are the eyes; the "ruler of the realm" is reason; "the fair palace door" is the mouth; and the "evil things" are the madman's fantasies. The poem is found in *The Fall of the House of Usher*.

Poe claimed that Longfellow's *Beleaguered City* was an imitation of *The Haunted Palace*. The former should be read in connection with the latter. Though some resemblance may be discerned, Longfellow must be acquitted of Poe's charge of plagiarism.

THE CONQUEROR WORM

1. This terrible lyric is also an allegory. The "theater" is the world, and the "play" human life. The "mimes" are men, created in the image of God, and are represented as the "mere puppets" of circumstance. The "Phantom chased for evermore" is happiness; but for all, the end is death and the grave.

THE RAVEN

1. This poem was first published in the New York *Evening Mirror*, January 29, 1845. "In our opinion," wrote the editor, N. P. Willis, "it is the most effective single example of 'fugitive poetry' ever published in this country; and unsurpassed in English poetry for subtle conception, masterly ingenuity of versification, and consistent sustaining of imaginative lift."

The story of *The Raven* is given in prose by Poe in his *Philosophy of Composition*, which contains the best analysis of its structure: "A raven, having learned by rote the single word, 'Nevermore,' and having escaped from the custody of its owner, is driven at midnight, through the violence of a storm, to seek admission at a window from which a light still gleams, — the chamber window of a student, occupied half in poring over a volume, half in dreaming of a beloved mistress deceased. The casement being thrown open at the fluttering of the bird's wings, the bird itself perches on the most convenient seat out of the immediate reach of the student, who, amused by the incident and the oddity of the visitor's demeanor, demands of it, in jest and without looking for a reply, its name. The raven addressed answers with its customary word, 'Nevermore' — a word which finds immediate echo in the melancholy heart of the student, who, giving utterance aloud to certain thoughts suggested by the occasion, is again startled by the fowl's repetition of 'Nevermore.' The student now guesses the state of the case, but is impelled, by the human thirst for self-torture, and in part by superstition, to propound such queries to the bird as will bring him, the lover, the most of the luxury of sorrow, through the anticipated answer, ' Nevermore.' "

2. As Poe explains, the raven is " emblematical of mournful and never-ending remembrance."

3. From the position of the bird it has been held that the shadow could not possibly fall upon the floor. But the author says : " *My* conception was that of the bracket candelabrum affixed against the wall, high up above the door and bust, as is often seen in the English palaces, and even in some of the better houses in New York."

NOTES TO SELECTIONS FROM HAYNE

For a general introduction to the following poems, see Chapter III. The selections are intended to exhibit the poet's various moods and themes.

THE WILL AND THE WING

1. This poem, which appeared in the volume of 1855 under the title *Aspirations*, gives expression to a strong literary impulse. It was genuine in sentiment, and its aspiring spirit and forceful utterance gave promise of no ordinary achievement.

2. An act or formula supposed to exert a magical influence or power.

> "Then, in one moment, she put forth the charm
> Of woven paces and of waving hands."
> — Tennyson's *Merlin and Vivien*.

Compare the first scene in *Faust* where the Earth-spirit comes in obedience to a "conquering spell."

3. Tantalus was a character of Greek mythology, who, for divulging the secret counsels of Zeus, was afflicted in the lower world with an insatiable thirst. He stood up to the chin in a lake, the waters of which receded whenever he tried to drink of them.

4. The poet evidently had in mind the lame man who was "laid daily at the gate of the temple which is called Beautiful." — *Acts* iii. 2.

5. A reference to the veil that hung before the Most Holy Place, or "inmost shrine," of the temple. Compare *Exodus* xxvi. 33.

MY STUDY

1. This sonnet, which appeared in the volume of 1859, reveals the retiring, meditative temper of the poet. To him

quiet reflection was more than action. He loved to dwell in spirit with the good and great of the past. The rude struggles of the market-place for wealth and power were repugnant to his refined and sensitive nature.

2. Something served for the refreshment of a person; here an intellectual feast fit for a prince.

3. Arcady, or Arcadia, is a place of ideal simplicity and contentment; so called from a picturesque district in Greece, which was noted for the simplicity and happiness of its people.

AËTHRA

1. This poem will serve to illustrate Hayne's skill in the use of blank verse. It is a piece of rare excellence and beauty. The name of the heroine is pronounced *Ee-thra*.

2. This migration occurred about 708 B.C.

3. Apollo was one of the major deities of Grecian mythology. He was regarded, among other things, as the god of song or minstrelsy, and also as the god of prophetic inspiration. The most celebrated oracle of Apollo was at Delphi.

4. A town in southern Italy, now Taranto. It was in ancient times a place of great commercial importance.

UNDER THE PINE

1. For the occasion of this poem, see page 61. The poet had a peculiar fondness for the pine, which in one of his poems he calls —

> " My sylvan darling! set 'twixt shade and sheen,
>   Soft as a maid, yet stately as a queen! "

It is the subject of a half-dozen poems, — *The Voice of the Pines, Aspect of the Pines, In the Pine Barrens, The Dryad of the Pine, The Pine's Mystery*, and *The Axe and the Pine*, — all of them in his happiest vein.

2. In *The Pine's Mystery* we read: —

> " Passion and mystery murmur through the leaves,
>   Passion and mystery, touched by deathless pain,
> Whose monotone of long, low anguish grieves
>   For something lost that shall not live again."

3. Hayne's very careful workmanship is rarely at fault ; but here there seems to be an infelicitous epithet that amounts to a sort of tautology. "Eyes ablaze" would necessarily "look forth with *burning* gaze."

CLOUD PICTURES

1. This poem illustrates the poet's method of dealing with Nature. He depicts its beauty as discerned by the artistic imagination. He is less concerned with the messages of Nature than with its lovely forms. This poem, in its felicitous word-painting, reminds us of Tennyson, though it would be difficult to find in the English poet so brilliant a succession of masterly descriptions.

With this poem may be compared Hayne's *Cloud Fantasies*, a sonnet that brings before us, with great vividness, the somber appearance of the clouds in autumn. See also *A Phantom in the Clouds*. No other of our poets has dwelt so frequently and so delightfully on the changing aspects of the sky.

Compare Shelley's *The Cloud*.

LYRIC OF ACTION

1. It is not often that Hayne assumed the hortatory tone found in this poem. In artistic temperament he was akin to Keats rather than to Longfellow. Even in his didactic poems, he is meditative and descriptive rather than hortatory. The artist in him hardly ever gave place to the preacher.

2. The seraph's name was Uriel, that is, God's Light. In *Revelation* (xix. 17) we read, "And I saw an angel standing in the sun." Milton calls him —

> "The Archangel Uriel — one of the seven
> Who in God's presence, nearest to his throne,
> Stand ready at command."
>
> *— Paradise Lost*, Book III, 648–650.

NOTES TO SELECTIONS FROM TIMROD

For a general introduction to the following selections, see Chapter IV. The poet's verse is perfectly clear. He prefers to

" Cling to the lowly and be content."

TOO LONG, O SPIRIT OF STORM

1. This poem, which first appeared in *Russell's Magazine*, exhibits one of Timrod's characteristics : he does not describe Nature for its own sake, as Hayne often does, but for the sake of some truth or lesson in relation to man. The lesson of this poem is that a life of uninterrupted ease and comfort is not favorable to the development of noble character.

A CRY TO ARMS

1. This selection illustrates the fierce energy of the poet's martial lyrics. Compare *Bannockburn* by Burns, which Carlyle said "should be sung with the throat of the whirlwind."

2. *Byre* is a cow-stable.

3. *Rack*, usually *wrack*, signifies ruin or destruction.

ODE

1. This lyric, which was sung on the occasion of decorating the graves of the Confederate dead in Magnolia Cemetery, Charleston, South Carolina, in 1867, has been much admired, especially the last stanza.

2. It is interesting to know that this prediction has been fulfilled. A monument of granite now stands above the dead.

3. *Behalf*, instead of *in behalf of*, is a rather hazardous construction.

4. A noble bronze figure of a color bearer on a granite pedestal now commemorates the fallen heroes.

FLOWER LIFE

1. This poem first appeared in the *Southern Literary Messenger* in 1851. The first stanza of this half-playful, half-serious piece, mentions the objects in which the poet most delighted.

2. This belief has been frequently held, and has some support from recent scientific experiments. But that this sentiency goes as far as the poet describes, is of course pure fancy.

3. The sibyls (Sybil is an incorrect form) were, according to ancient mythology, prophetic women. The sibylline leaves or books contained their teachings, and were preserved with the utmost care in Rome. The sibyl of Cumæ conducted Æneas through the under world, as narrated in the sixth book of Virgil's *Æneid*.

SONNET

1. This sonnet expresses the poet's creed, to which his practice was confirmed. This fact imparts unusual simplicity to his verse — a simplicity that strikes us all the more at the present time, when an over-refinement of thought and expression is in vogue.

SONNET

1. This sonnet, on the commonest of all poetic themes, treats of love in a deep, serious way. It is removed as far as possible from the sentimental.

2. This line reminds us of a well-known passage in Byron: —

> " Man's love is of man's life a thing apart;
>   'Tis woman's whole existence.   Man may range
>   The court, camp, church, the vessel and the mart;
>   Sword, gown, gain, glory, offer in exchange
>   Pride, fame, ambition, to fill up his heart,
>   And few there are whom these cannot estrange."

3. This is the divine ideal, the realization of which will bring the true "Golden Age." "God is love; and he that dwelleth in love dwelleth in God, and God in him." — 1 *John* iv. 16.

THE SUMMER BOWER

1. This poem first appeared in the *Southern Literary Messenger* in 1852. It will serve to show Timrod's manner of using blank verse. It will be observed that "a lesson" is again the principal thing.

2. This recalls the closing lines of Longfellow's *Sunrise on the Hills* : —

> " If thou art worn and hard beset
> With sorrows that thou wouldst forget,
> If thou wouldst read a lesson that will keep
> Thy heart from fainting and thy soul from sleep,
> Go to the woods and hills!　No tears
> Dim the sweet look that Nature wears."

3. Compare the following lines from Bryant's *Thanatopsis* : —

> " To him who in the love of Nature holds
> Communion with her visible forms, she speaks
> A various language; for his gayer hours
> She has a voice of gladness, and a smile
> And eloquence of beauty, and she glides
> Into his darker musings, with a mild
> And healing sympathy, that steals away
> Their sharpness, ere he is aware."

NOTES TO SELECTIONS FROM LANIER

For a general introduction to Lanier's poetry, see Chapter V.

THE SONG OF THE CHATTAHOOCHEE

1. This poem was first published in *Scott's Magazine*, Atlanta, Georgia, from which it is here taken. It at once became popular, and was copied in many newspapers throughout the South. It was subsequently revised, and the changes, which are pointed out below, are interesting as showing the development of the poet's artistic sense.

The singularly rapid and musical lilt of this poem may be readily traced to its sources. It is due to the skillful use of short vowels, liquid consonants, internal rhyme, and constant alliteration. These are matters of technique which Lanier studiously employed throughout his poetry.

This poem abounds in seeming irregularities of meter. The fundamental measure is iambic tetrameter, as in the line —

"The rushes cried, *Abide, abide*";

but trochees, dactyls, or anapests are introduced in almost every line, yet without interfering with the time element of the verse. These irregularities were no doubt introduced in order to increase the musical effects.

2. As may be seen by reference to a map, the Chattahoochee rises in Habersham County, in northeastern Georgia, and in its southwesterly course passes through the adjoining county of Hall. Its entire length is about five hundred miles.

3. Changed in the revision to "I hurry amain," with the present tense of the following verbs. The pronoun "his" in line 6 becomes "my."

4. This line was changed to —

> "The laving laurel turned my tide."

5. In this line the use of a needless antiquated form may be fairly questioned. In the revised form " win " is changed to " work."

6. "Barred" is changed to " did bar " in the revision — a doubtful gain.

7. The preceding four lines show a decided poetic gain in the revised form : —

> " And many a luminous jewel lone —
>   Crystals clear or a-cloud with mist,
>   Ruby, garnet, and amethyst —
> Made lures with the lightnings of streaming stone."

8. The revised form, with an awkward pause after the first foot, and also a useless antiquated phrase, reads —

> "Avail! I am fain for to water the plain."

9. Changed to "myriad of flowers."

10. " Final " was changed to " lordly " with fine effect.

This poem challenges comparison with other pieces of similar theme. It lacks the exquisite workmanship of Tennyson's *The Brook*, with its incomparable onomatopœic effects : —

> " I chatter over stony ways,
>   In little sharps and trebles;
> I bubble into eddying bays,
>   I babble on the pebbles."

It should be compared with Hayne's *The River* and also with his *The Meadow Brook* : —

> " Tinkle, tinkle, tinkle,
>   Hark! the tiny swell;
> Of wavelets softly, silverly
>   Toned like a fairy bell,
> Whose every note, dropped sweetly
>   In mellow glamour round,
> Echo hath caught and harvested
>   In airy sheaves of sound!"

But *The Song of the Chattahoochee* has what the other poems lack, — a lofty moral purpose. The noble stream consciously resists the allurements of pleasure to heed "the voices of duty," and this spirit imparts to it a greater dignity and weight.

THE CRYSTAL

1. This poem appeared in *The Independent*, July 15, 1880, from which it is taken. It illustrates the intellectual rather than the musical side of Lanier's genius. It is purely didactic, and thought rather than melody guides the poet's pen. The meter is quite regular, — an unusual thing in our author's most characteristic work.

It shows Lanier's use of pentameter blank verse, — a use that is somewhat lacking in ease and clearness. The first sentence is longer than that of *Paradise Lost*, without Milton's unity and force. Such ponderous sentences are all too frequent in Lanier, and as a result he is sometimes obscure. Repeated readings are necessary to take in the full meaning of his best work.

This poem, though not bearing the distinctive marks of his genius, is peculiarly interesting for two reasons, — it gives us an insight into his wide range of reading and study, and it exhibits his penetration and sanity as a critic. In the long list of great names he never fails to put his finger on the vulnerable spot. Frequently he is exceedingly felicitous, as when he speaks of "rapt Behmen, rapt too far," or of "Emerson, Most wise, that yet, in finding Wisdom, lost Thy Self sometimes."

2. It will be remembered that Lanier was a careful student of Shakespeare, on whom he lectured to private classes in Baltimore.

3. See second part of *King Henry IV*, iii. 1. The passage which the poet had in mind begins : —

> " How many thousand of my poorest subjects
> Are at this hour asleep ! "

4. See *The Two Gentlemen of Verona*.

5. These characters are found as follows : Viola in *Twelfth Night* ; Julia in *The Two Gentlemen of Verona* ; Portia in *The Merchant of Venice* ; and Rosalind in *As You Like It*.

6. Referring to the well-known catalogue of ships in the Second Book of the Illiad : —

> " My song to fame shall give
> The chieftains, and enumerate their ships."

It is in this passage in particular that Homer is supposed to nod.

7. It will be recalled that Paris, son of Priam, king of Troy, persuaded Helen, the fairest of women and wife of King Menelaus of Greece, to elope with him to Troy. This incident gave rise to the famous Trojan War.

8. Socrates (469–399 B.C.) was an Athenian philosopher, of whom Cicero said that he " brought down philosophy from the heavens to the earth." His teachings are preserved in Xenophon's *Memorabilia* and Plato's *Dialogues*.

9. That is to say, his needless austerity was as much affected as the dandy's excessive and ostentatious refinement.

10. Buddha, meaning *the enlightened one*, was Prince Siddhartha of Hindustan, who died about 477 B.C. He was the founder of the Buddhist religion, which teaches that the supreme attainment of mankind is Nirvana or extinction. This doctrine naturally follows from the Buddhist assumption that life is hopelessly evil. Many of the moral precepts of Buddhism are closely akin to those of Christianity.

11. Dante Alighieri (1265–1321), a native of Florence, is the greatest poet of Italy and one of the greatest poets of the world. His immortal poem, *The Divine Comedy*, is divided into three parts — " Hell," " Purgatory," and " Paradise."

12. This is a reference to the wars among the angels, which ended with the expulsion of Satan and his hosts from heaven, as related in the sixth book of *Paradise Lost*. This criticism of Milton is as just as it is felicitous.

13. Æschylus (525–456 B.C.) was the father of Greek tragedy. He presents *destiny* in its sternest aspects. His *Prometheus Bound* has been translated by Mrs. Browning, and his *Agamemnon* by Robert Browning — two dramas that exhibit his grandeur and power at their best.

14. Lucretius (about 95–51 B.C.) was the author of a didactic poem in six books entitled *De Rerum Natura*. It is Epicurean in morals and atheistic in philosophy. At the same

time, as a work of art, it is one of the most perfect poems that have descended to us from antiquity.

15. Marcus Aurelius Antoninus (121–180 A.D.), one of the best emperors of Rome, was a noble Stoic philosopher. His *Meditations* is regarded by John Stuart Mill as almost equal to the Sermon on the Mount in moral elevation.

16. Thomas a Kempis (1379–1471) was the author of the famous *Imitation of Christ* in which, as Dean Milman says, " is gathered and concentered all that is elevating, passionate, profoundly pious in all the older mystics." No other book, except the Bible, has been so often translated and printed.

17. Epictetus (born about 50 A.D.) was a Stoic philosopher, many of whose moral teachings resemble those of Christianity. But he unduly emphasized renunciation, and wished to restrict human aspiration to the narrow limits of the attainable.

18. Jacob Behmen, or Böhme (1575–1624), was a devout mystic philosopher, whose speculations, containing much that was beautiful and profound, sometimes passed the bounds of intelligibility.

19. Emanuel Swedenborg (1688–1772) was a Swedish philosopher and theologian. His principal work, *Arcana Cœlestia*, is made up of profound speculations and spiritualistic extravagance. He often oversteps the bounds of sanity.

20. William Langland, or Langley (about 1332–1400), a disciple of Wycliffe, was a poet, whose *Vision of Piers Plowman*, written in strong, alliterative verse, describes, in a series of nine visions, the manifold corruptions of society, church, and state in England.

21. Cædmon (lived about 670) was a cowherd attached to the monastery of Whitby in England. Later he became a poet, and wrote on Scripture themes in his native Anglo-Saxon. His *Paraphrase*, is, next to *Beowulf*, the oldest Anglo-Saxon poem in existence.

22. Lanier was deeply religious, but his beliefs were broader than any creed. In *Remonstrance* he exclaims, —

> " Opinion, let me alone : I am not thine.
> Prim Creed, with categoric point, forbear
> To feature me my Lord by rule and line."

Yet, as shown in the conclusion of *The Crystal* he had an exalted sense of the unapproachable beauty of the life and teachings of Christ. His tenderest poem is *A Ballad of Trees and the Master :* —

> " Into the woods my Master went,
> Clean forspent, forspent.
> Into the woods my Master came,
> Forspent with love and shame.
> But the olives they were not blind to Him,
> The little gray leaves were kind to Him ;
> The thorn-tree had a mind to Him,
> When into the woods He came.

> " Out of the woods my Master went,
> And He was well content.
> Out of the woods my Master came,
> Content with death and shame.
> When Death and Shame would woo Him last,
> From under the trees they drew Him last :
> 'Twas on a tree they slew Him — last
> When out of the woods He came."

SUNRISE

1. This poem was first published in *The Independent*, December 14, 1882, from which it is here taken. The editor said, "This poem, we do not hesitate to say, is one of the few great poems that have been written on this side the ocean." With this judgment there will be general agreement on the part of appreciative readers. On the emotional side, it may be said to reach the high-water mark of poetic achievement in this country. Its emotion at times reaches the summits of poetic rapture ; a little more, and it would have passed into the boundary of hysterical ecstasy.

The circumstances of its composition possess a melancholy interest. It was Lanier's last and greatest poem. He penciled it a few months before his death when he was too feeble to raise his food to his mouth and when a burning fever was consuming him. Had he not made this supreme effort, American literature would be the poorer.

This poem exhibits, in a high degree, the poet's love for Nature. Indeed, most of his great pieces — *The Marshes of Glynn*, *Clover*, *Corn*, and others — are inspired by the sights and sounds of Nature. *Sunrise*, in general tone and style, closely resembles *The Marshes of Glynn*.

The musical theories of Lanier in relation to poetry find their highest exemplification in *Sunrise*. It is made up of all the poetic feet — iambics, trochees, dactyls, anapests — so that it almost defies any attempt at scansion. But the melody of the verse never fails; equality of time is observed, along with a rich use of alliteration and assonance.

The poem may be easily analyzed; and a distinct notation of its successive themes may be helpful to the young reader. Its divisions are marked by its irregular stanzas. It consists of fifteen parts as follows: 1. The call of the marshes to the poet in his slumbers, and his awaking. 2. He comes as a lover to the live-oaks and marshes. 3. His address to the "man-bodied tree," and the "cunning green leaves." 4. His petition for wisdom and for a prayer of intercession. 5. The stirring of the owl. 6. Address to the "reverend marsh, distilling silence." 7. Description of the full tide. 8. "The bow-and-string tension of beauty and silence." 9. The motion of dawn. 10. The golden flush of the eastern sky. 11. The sacramental marsh at worship. 12. The slow rising of the sun above the sea horizon. 13. Apostrophe to heat. 14. The worker must pass from the contemplation of this splendor to his toil. 15. The poet's inextinguishable adoration of the sun.

2. "Gospeling glooms" means glooms that convey to the sensitive spirit sweet messages of good news.

3. Lanier continually attributes personality to the objects of Nature, and places them in tender relations to man. Here the little leaves become —

> "Friendly, sisterly, sweetheart leaves,"

as a few lines before they were "little masters."

In *Individuality* we read, —

> "Sail on, sail on, fair cousin Cloud."

And in *Corn* there is a passage of great tenderness : —

> " The leaves that wave against my cheek caress
>   Like women's hands ; the embracing boughs express
>   A subtlety of mighty tenderness ;
> The copse-depths into little noises start,
> That sound anon like beatings of a heart,
> Anon like talk 'twixt lips not far apart."

4. This passage is Wordsworthian in spirit. Nature is regarded as a teacher who suggests or reveals ineffable things. Lanier might have said, as did Wordsworth, —

> " To me the meanest flower that blows can give
>   Thoughts that do often lie too deep for tears."

5. Lanier had a lively and vigorous imagination, which is seen in his use of personification and metaphor. In this poem almost every object — trees, leaves, marsh, streams, sun, heat — is personified. This same fondness for personification may be observed in his other characteristic poems.

In the use of metaphor it may be doubted whether the poet is always so happy. There is sometimes inaptness or remoteness in his resemblances. To liken the flaming heavens to a beehive, and the rising sun to a bee issuing from the " hive-hole," can hardly be said to add dignity to the description. In *Clover* men are clover heads, which the Course-of-things, as an ox, browses upon : —

> " This cool, unasking Ox
> Comes browsing o'er my hills and vales of Time,
> And thrusts me out his tongue, and curls it, sharp,
> And sicklewise, about my poets' heads,
> And twists them in . . .
>   and champs and chews,
> With slantly-churning jaws and swallows down."

6. The deities of Olympus, being immortal, have no need of strenuous haste. They may well move from pleasure to pleasure with stately leisure.

NOTES TO SELECTIONS FROM FATHER RYAN

For a general introduction to Father Ryan's poetry, see Chapter VI.

SONG OF THE MYSTIC

1. As stated in the sketch of Father Ryan, this poem strikes the keynote to his verse. It therefore properly opens his volume of poems. It became popular on its first publication, and was copied in various papers. It is here taken from the *Religious Herald*, Richmond, Virginia.

2. The location of *The Valley of Silence* is given in the last stanza.

3. This poem may be taken, in a measure, as autobiographic. In this stanza, and the two following ones, the poet refers to that period of his life before he resolved to consecrate himself to the priesthood.

4. This indicates the general character of his poetry. Inspired in *The Valley of Silence*, it is sad, meditative, mystical, religious.

5. Perhaps every poet has this experience. There come to him elusive glimpses of truth and beauty which are beyond the grasp of speech. As some one has sung : —

> "Sometimes there rise, from deeps unknown,
>   Before my inmost gaze,
> Far brighter scenes than earth has shown
>   In morning's orient blaze;
> I try to paint the visions bright,
> But, oh, their glories turn to night!"

THE CONQUERED BANNER

1. This poem was first published in Father Ryan's paper, the *Banner of the South*, March 21, 1868, from which it is here taken. Coming so soon after the close of the Civil War, it touched the Southern heart.

2. For a criticism of the versification of this stanza, see the chapter on Father Ryan.

3. This note of pardon, in keeping with the poet's priestly character, is found in several of his lyrics referring to the war. In spite of his strong Southern feeling, there is no unrelenting bitterness. Thus, in *The Prayer of the South*, which appeared a week later, we read : —

> "Father, I kneel 'mid ruin, wreck, and grave, —
>   A desert waste, where all was erst so fair, —
> And for my children and my foes I crave
>   Pity and pardon.   Father, hear my prayer!"

4. This was the poet's feeling in 1868.   In a similar strain we read in *The Prayer of the South :* —

> "My heart is filled with anguish deep and vast!
>   My hopes are buried with my children's dust!
> My joys have fled, my tears are flowing fast!
>   In whom, save Thee, our Father, shall I trust?"

Happily the poet lived to see a new order of things — an era in which vain regrets gave place to energetic courage, hope, and endeavor.

THE SWORD OF ROBERT LEE

1. This poem first appeared in the *Banner of the South*, April 4, 1868, and, like the preceding one, has been very popular in the South.

2. Father Ryan felt great admiration for General Lee, who has remained in the South the popular hero of the war.   In the last of his *Sentinel Songs*, the poet-priest pays a beautiful tribute to the stainless character of the Confederate leader : —

> "Go, Glory, and forever guard
>   Our chieftain's hallowed dust;
> And Honor, keep eternal ward,
>   And Fame, be this thy trust!
> Go, with your bright emblazoned scroll
>   And tell the years to be,
> The first of names to flash your roll
>   Is ours — great Robert Lee."

DEATH

1. This poem was first published in the *Banner of the South*, April 25, 1868. It illustrates the profounder themes on which the poet loved to dwell, and likewise the Christian faith by which they were illumined.

2. This mournful view of life appears frequently in Father Ryan's poems. In *De Profundis*, for example, we read: —

> "All the hours are full of tears —
>   O my God! woe are we!
> Grief keeps watch in brightest eyes —
> Every heart is strung with fears,
>   Woe are we! woe are we!
> All the light hath left the skies,
> And the living, awe-struck crowds
> See above them only clouds,
> And around them only shrouds."

PRESENTIMENT

1. This poem, as the two preceding ones, is taken from the *Banner of the South*, where it appeared June 13, 1868. It affords a glimpse of the tragical romance of the poet's life. The voice that he hears is that of "Ethel," the lost love of his youth. Her memory never left him. In the poem entitled *What?* it is again her spirit voice that conveys to his soul an ineffable word.

2. This desire for death occurs in several poems, as *When?* and *Rest*. In the latter poem it is said: —

> " 'Twas always so; when but a child I laid
>   On mother's breast
> My wearied little head — e'en then I prayed
>   As now — for rest."

NIGHT THOUGHTS

1. This poem is taken from the *Banner of the South*, where it appeared June 29, 1870. In the volume of collected poems the title is changed to *The Rosary of my Tears*.

2. "Brave" is changed to "lone" in the poet's revision.